When Any Time Was Train Time

The Petersburg station operator's work station showing telegraph key, train
order phone, clock, lantern, flags, etc. When this station closed, it was relocated
to Kitchener's Doon Heritage Crossroads, where this photograph was taken.

When Any Time Was Train Time

by Elizabeth A. Willmot

A Boston Mills Press Book

Canadian Cataloguing Publication Data

Willmot, Elizabeth A.
  When any time was train time

ISBN 1-55046-056-0

1. Railroads - Ontario - History. 2. Railroads - Ontario - Stations
- History. I. Title.

HE2809.05W55 1992   385'.09713   C92-093906-6

All photographs by Elizabeth A. Willmot unless otherwise indicated.
Design *George W. Roth, Polygon Design Limited*
Edited *Noel Hudson*
Typography *Dobbie Graphics*
Printed in Canada

First published in 1992 by
Stoddart Publishing Co. Limited
34 Lesmill Road
Toronto, Canada
M3B 2T6

A BOSTON MILLS PRESS BOOK
The Boston Mills Press
132 Main Street
Erin, Ontario
NOB 1TO

The publisher gratefully acknowledges the support of the Canada Council,
Ontario Ministry of Culture and Communications, Ontario Arts Council
and Ontario Publishing Centre in the development of writing and publishing
in Canada.

Winners of the
Heritage Canada
Communications Award

American Association
for State and Local History
Award Winner

Page 1 photo caption
Station order board.

In Memory of Bill

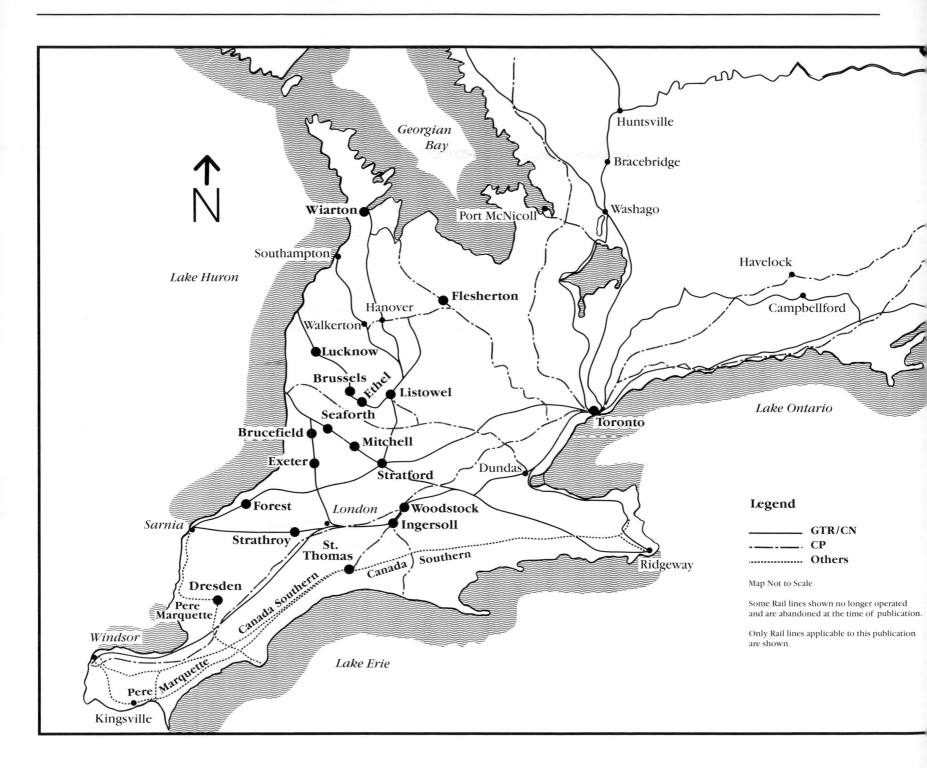

Georgian Bay

Lake Huron

Lake Ontario

Lake Erie

Wiarton

Southampton

Port McNicoll

Huntsville

Bracebridge

Washago

Havelock

Campbellford

Flesherton

Hanover

Walkerton

Lucknow

Brussels **Ethel** **Listowel**

Seaforth

Brucefield **Mitchell**

Exeter

Stratford Dundas

Forest *London* **Woodstock**

Sarnia **Ingersoll**

Strathroy **St. Thomas** *Canada Southern*

Toronto

Ridgeway

Dresden

Pere Marquette

Windsor *Pere Marquette* *Canada Southern*

Lake Erie

Pere

Kingsville

Legend

	GTR/CN
	CP
	Others

Map Not to Scale

Some Rail lines shown no longer operated and are abandoned at the time of publication.

Only Rail lines applicable to this publication are shown.

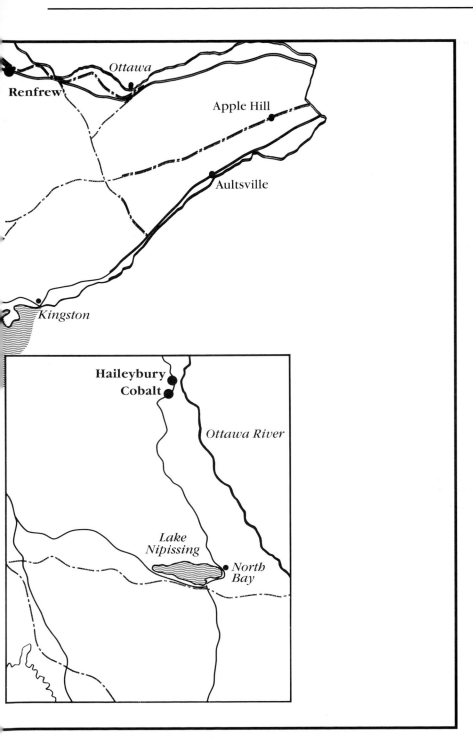

CONTENTS

ACKNOWLEDGEMENTS

I wish to thank the many people throughout Ontario who shared their stories with me and who guided me to others whose recollections of railways are included in this book. I am particularly grateful to the following people: Brian Moreau of CN Public Affairs, who has supported my projects for years; Don Spearman, editor, in Dresden; Frank Kelly, retired CN station agent at Mitchell; Gordon Wright of Seaforth; the Elgin Historical Society of St. Thomas; John Hoyle, railway historian, in Forest; writer Harry Hinchley from Renfrew; Eleanor Gardhouse of Woodstock; the late Andy MacLean, editor, Seaforth; my good friend the late Len Appleyard, railway photographer; and another very dear friend, Herbert Stitt, retired CPR engineer and author of *I Remember*. Finally, a special tribute to my dear husband, the late Bill Kettlewell, artist, equestrian and sculptor, who persuaded me to write this book and to whom it is dedicated.

INTRODUCTION

When I took my first photographs of steam locomotives and railway stations, Ontario was still a meshwork of railway lines and any time was train time.

You could travel almost anywhere by train in those days. The two big railways were the CPR and CNR, but I preferred trips on those less important lines that seemed to meander through Ontario, lines whose stations had been the very core of their small communities for more than a century. These local trains usually consisted of two or three old coaches, a baggage car, an engine and a friendly crew.

Hundreds of stations were built all over Ontario, but each one had its own characteristics (though faded boxcar red with cream trim around the windows was a popular colour scheme). Many handsome stations were built of fieldstone or limestone and were expected to last forever.

How wonderful it would be if a diary had been kept at each country railway station! So much of our history occurred at these stations.

We have been losing an irreplaceable chapter in our history in recent years with the closing of old railway lines. Very few rural stations still survive. Some have become restaurants or museums; others have simply been padlocked and will inevitably become targets for vandals.

Tales are still told about the days when any time was train time, but like the old stations themselves, the tellers of these tales are becoming increasingly difficult to find.

A southbound CN passenger train slows for mail-handlers at Brucefield in the
1920s. This station was built by the London, Huron & Bruce Railway.
Photograph circa 1922.
Gordon Wright collection

BRUCEFIELD

In the 1880s the London, Huron & Bruce Railway's head office in London had a superintendent with a great sense of humour. When a Mr. Bruce Field came to him looking for a job, he promptly appointed the man to the station agent's position in the village of Brucefield!

This station was just a small, white frame building about six miles south of the town of Clinton. In a twelve-foot-square section in the southwest corner of the station was the waiting room, with three benches for passengers, who were kept warm in winter by an oval-shaped potbelly stove. Posters advertising country fairs and the Canadian National Exhibition were tacked on the walls. The station agent worked in his small ticket office, where he also operated the telegrapher's key. Two-thirds of the building, on the north end, were used as a freight shed.

Despite its size, the Brucefield station was a busy spot from the day it opened in 1876. In that first year, the station's income from freight and cattle shipments and passenger ticket sales was over nine thousand dollars.

Perhaps it was the novelty which attracted so many young men to seek employment on the railways in the 1800s. It certainly was not the wages! A station agent in Brucefield in 1899 received a mere forty dollars a month plus his accommodation, heat and light. Hours were long and irregular. In addition to selling tickets and being a skilled telegrapher, the station agent was expected to keep attractive gardens around his station, shovel snow from the platform, and have a sympathetic ear for everyone's problems. The Brucefield station agent's most difficult duty during the First World War was personally delivering telegrams informing Brucefield families of the death of a son or husband.

The Brucefield railway station and its associated buildings represented the very heart of the community until the Depression of the 1930s.

Four passenger trains ran between London and Wingham, and a great many freight trains. Service was good.

Today, if you drive across the tracks at edge of the village, rarely do you have to stop for a train. There hasn't been a passenger train on the line since 1941. However, since April 1992, freight trains operated by the Goderich & Exeter Railway travel over the line three times a week.

When the passenger station was of no further use in Brucefield, it was loaded onto a truck and moved up to Clinton, where it serves as a meeting hall for Orangemen. Soon the Brucefield station's sheds disappeared, and the cattle pens, and the section foreman's house and shanty.

There is an eerie and disturbing quietness about abandoned or infrequently used railway tracks. Knee-high wildflowers and grass line the tracks in summertime. If you pick your way along the rotting ties north of the site of the Brucefield railway station, you will discover an old padlocked switch almost hidden in the dense growth. This switch once controlled a spur line to one of the mills built by an early settler. But today just a few feet of the spur remain, leading nowhere.

Early Brucefield businesses depended on the railway for shipping and supplies. William Scott's grain elevator was a favourite gathering place for farmers. A windmill built on top of the elevator provided its power until Hydro was brought to Brucefield in 1927. Scott, one of the original settlers, supplied cordwood for the railway when wood-burning steam engines were still used. It was a profitable business.

George Beatty operated a coal business just south of Scott's mill. A large lumber and coal business was owned by the Mustard family, who came to Canada from Scotland in the 1830s. Their descendants still live in Brucefield. Sandy Mustard's sawmill piped steam to a nearby stave mill, where barrel staves were steamed into shape.

Cattle-shipping day was usually Saturday, and it always drew a good crowd of spectators. Cattle buyers William Taylor and Charles Reid would be at the farms before daylight, bargaining with the farmers. Cattle and hogs were brought to the stock pens at the north end of the station, then weighed and loaded onto Toronto-bound trains.

Jack and Alex Mustard, and many of their friends rode the south-bound morning train to attend high school in Exeter, twelve miles away. The railway's rate for students was forty tickets for three dollars. For many years, the same crew worked on the morning train. Conductor "Mac" MacDonald was popular with all the passengers, and no one worried about his inclination to "bend an elbow." When Mac was having one of his "jolly" days, there were some hilarious moments for his passengers.

Ross Scott remembered spending a lot of time down at the Brucefield station and at his grandfather's grain elevator. The two station agents he remembered well were Mr. Rose and a good-humoured Englishman, Mr. Prime, who had a great bushy beard and always had a joke to share.

When Ross Scott was in his teen years, it was regarded as a sign of manhood when the village boys began walking their girlfriends to the station after Sunday-evening church services. When the last train of the day had gone through, the evening of hand-holding was over and you strolled slowly home.

The history of Brucefield's railway station would be incomplete if the mystery of the missing station agent were omitted. One day, for no apparent reason, Brucefield's agent simply vanished. Newspapers were filled with speculation for weeks. No money was missing from the station and all the agent's personal effects were left in place at his boarding house. He was well-liked and a respected employee. When two letters from a girl in a neighbouring community were found in his room, it was hoped they would provide a clue. The amorous correspondent had become infatuated after seeing the handsome station agent from the window of her train when it had stopped in Brucefield. Courageously, she wrote, with flowery phrases, inviting the agent to share an evening of sleigh-riding, begging him not to think unkindly of her. The girl's name was never revealed, but editors and clergymen published scathing letters about her boldness. The mystery remained unsolved, however, and the story continued to be good parlour conversation for many years.

BRUSSELS

The coming of the railway to a pioneer community symbolized prosperity and the promise of a great future. But for Brussels' first settler, William Ainlay, it was also a time for reflection. While standing with the crowd awaiting the first train's arrival on July 1, 1873, no doubt Ainlay recalled his lonely arrival in 1852. At the time, there was no transportation in this uninhabited part of Huron County, and the only road was a vague trail through the forest. William Ainlay had visualized a settlement growing at this spot on a branch of the Maitland River. The land was fertile and the forest untouched. He cleared a patch of ground and built a cabin, then returned to Perth County to persuade his neighbours to join him in creating a new community. These new settlers arrived the following year, and the land they staked out for their future village was called Ainlayville.

Not everyone was happy with the chosen name, and when the first post office was established, it was called Dingle (which was also the name of the first pub). Further confusion arose when the railway station was built in 1873. A curious custom allowed the building contractor to choose the name for the station. The signboard he erected on the new station read "Brussels," a name that settled the twenty-year debate.

The village was all dressed up on that first day of July 1873. No one in attendance had ever taken part in the formal opening of a railway, and few had even seen a train. The arrival of the first train on the newly built extension of the Wellington, Grey & Bruce Railway was an occasion that called for Sunday clothes and a holiday for everyone!

A Seaforth newspaper reporter covered the event with enthusiasm: "The Village was handsomely decorated with flags, banners, arches and evergreens. The main arch extended across Main Street from Mr. Leckie's store to Hall's Hotel. On the top of the arch in handsome letters was the word 'Progress.' Suspended from the centre and surrounded by a wreath of evergreens were the letters 'W.G. & B.R.,' and along the sides, 'Stephenson' and 'James Watt' [early pioneers of the age of steam]."

Another archway on the main street near the station carried the word WELCOME in large letters. The gaily decorated village was described as "imposing, attractive, and well calculated to inspire admiration of visitors."

John Leckie, the village reeve, greeted the railway officials when they stepped onto the platform from their special coach. His welcoming speech was acknowledged by Mr. McGiverin, president of the railway.

A colourful parade was formed at the station and led by the Wellington Battalion Band. Uniformed members of the Brussels Volunteer Company followed the band, and behind them came horse-drawn carriages transporting railway officials, their wives, and local dignitaries. Villagers and visitors joined the parade as it proceeded beneath the floral arches along the main street and continued on to Vanstone's new mill, where the banquet was to be held.

Ceremony officials were seated at a table across the front of the long room, and four tables extending the length of the room accommodated the large group of guests. The meal was described as a "bounteous feast." Many speeches were made and the usual "loyal and patriotic toasts" followed the dinner. The newspaper commented upon the "large number of ladies who graced the occasion with their presence," as it was customary for ladies to express their disapproval of the robust toasting at these affairs by refraining from attending.

The impact of the new railway in Brussels was apparent within months. Large shipments of squared timber were among the most profitable exports. By 1875 the population had grown to more than one thousand residents. Four excellent hotels catered to the travellers who arrived on the six daily passenger trains.

The railway came to Brussels on July 1, 1873. By 1875 the town's population had grown to over one thousand residents, and four hotels catered to the travellers who arrived on the six daily passenger trains. Passenger service was discontinued on November 1, 1970. Today the station serves as a lawn-bowlers' clubhouse.

Brussels became nationally known for its prize-winning steam-powered engines, which were manufactured at J.D. Ronald's Brussels' Steam Fire Engine Works. The village was also the only community in Huron County with a corset factory!

It became apparent in the 1960s that railway passenger service along the branch lines was coming to a close. A combination passenger-baggage car was put into service in 1963, but finally, on November 1, 1970, passenger service was discontinued. There was a general feeling of loss and disappointment in the community when the popular old station was boarded up. However, a happy ending came about when Brussels' railway station was moved down the road to the lawn-bowling club, where, freshly painted in the traditional boxcar red, it now serves as the bowlers' new clubhouse.

Grand Trunk station clock.

COBALT AND HAILEYBURY

Fortune hunters shared a common dream in 1903 when they scrambled aboard northbound Temiskaming & Northern Ontario Railway trains headed for a place called Cobalt, about a hundred miles north of North Bay. The wild gold-rush days in the Yukon and California had nothing on the sudden rush up to Cobalt, where silver had been discovered.

It all began in September 1903. The railway was opening a new Canadian frontier with a line beginning at North Bay and ending at Hudson Bay. Fred LaRose, a railway blacksmith, is said to have thrown his hammer at a fox peering at him from behind a rock. He missed the fox but struck what became the world's richest silver mine. The geologist who confirmed LaRose's find erected a signboard at this spot on the unfinished railway tracks. It read: "Cobalt Station, T&NO Railway." Cobalt was born and the rush began! Prospectors and promoters couldn't get up to Cobalt fast enough. Tomorrow they would be millionaires!

Five miles north of Cobalt, at Haileybury, another dream came closer to reality when the T&NO tracks reached that little settlement in 1903. For C.C. Farr, founder of Haileybury and one of the keenest promoters of the railroad, the sound of that first train whistle was indeed heavenly music.

There were no settlements in this region when C.C. Farr immigrated to Canada. Drawn by the mystery of this unexplored area, he joined the Hudson's Bay Company and was posted to Fort Timiskaming in 1874. In 1889 he bought property on Lake Timiskaming, where he visualized the growth of a prosperous farming community. He persuaded friends from England to join him, and eventually lumbermen and farmers from the Ottawa Valley and Muskoka also moved to the little settlement which Farr called Haileybury, for the school he had attended in England. A year after the discovery of silver in Cobalt, Haileybury's population numbered four hundred. By 1907 there were four thousand residents in the incorporated municipality.

Because Cobalt's houses were few and of poor quality, Haileybury became home to a great many prospectors and engineers. The well-stocked bars in Haileybury's four hotels were a great drawing card to miners from Cobalt, as it was illegal to sell liquor within five miles of working mine sites. Haileybury's hotels were conveniently five and half miles from Cobalt.

Miners and most residents in the two communities were delighted when an electric streetcar line was built in 1912. Half-hour service between Cobalt and Haileybury was available from 6 a.m. to 11 p.m.

Cobalt's Timiskaming & Northern Ontario Railway station, built in 1910, provided a greatly needed touch of refinement in this makeshift settlement. The station was designed by John M. Lyle, a prominent Toronto architect (one of the three architects who later designed Toronto's Union Station, which opened in 1927).

Covering the long brick building is a gracefully curved, hipped roof. Telegraphers used the space in the upper portion of the station. On the main floor were a ticket office, a general waiting room, and a private waiting room for ladies. Among the interior's interesting features were its red brick walls and its wooden ceiling supported by massive timber roof trusses. The station was regarded as one of the most handsome and imaginative examples of station architecture of the period.

When the first section of the T&NO Railway's line was completed and officially opened between North Bay and New Liskeard on January 16, 1905, Haileybury's station was still a wooden boxcar. J.H. Shibley was Haileybury's first station agent.

A fine brick railway station replaced the old boxcar and soon became a town beauty spot. The magnificent lawns and flower gardens surrounding the station were supplied and tended by local horticulturists.

Cobalt's Temiskaming & Northern Ontario Railway station, built in 1910, was designed by architect John Lyle, one of three architects who designed Toronto's Union Station. This photo was taken in 1980.

In 1905, when the Temiskaming & Northern Ontario Railway completed its line between North Bay and New Liskeard, Haileybury's station was still a wooden boxcar. A fine brick station replaced the boxcar but was one of seven hundred buildings destroyed in the tragic fire of 1922. The station pictured here was built following that fire and is still in use.

Unfortunately, the station was one of the seven hundred buildings destroyed in the tragic fire of October 4, 1922. A new railway station was built and is still in use.

Two of T&NO's best-known passengers were a pair of dogs. "O Dawg" was the constant companion of Haileybury's C.C. Farr, and "Cobalt" belonged to a Cobalt resident who travelled frequently to Toronto. While in the city, Cobalt and his master stayed at the King Edward Hotel. The hotel's kitchen staff often sent plates of tasty leftovers up to Cobalt's room. Because he enjoyed the trip and treats so much, Cobalt began taking the trip unaccompanied. He was always welcomed at the hotel and miraculously knew which train would take him home! "O Dawg" was less venturesome and favoured the short trip to Cobalt. But he insisted on having a seat to himself and would growl and bare his teeth if a passenger sat down beside him.

The boom-town atmosphere of Cobalt and Haileybury waned during the 1920s when several of Cobalt's mines were closed and many miners moved on. But even today tourists sense a frontier-town feeling when they see the mine shafts, the small frame houses bunched together, the occasional false-front store, and the excellent museum with its records of Cobalt's early days.

Haileybury founder C.C. Farr, who died in 1914, would have been heartbroken if he had lived to see his town almost wiped out by the 1922 fire. He had seen Haileybury prosper, with fine homes, four hotels, his own newspaper, *The Haileyburian*, a mining school, churches, a hospital, library, golf course, and a railway that had brought settlers to his community.

A 1909 postcard showing the Cobalt station from the south end.

DRESDEN

While almost every little hamlet in southern Ontario was trying to lure railroads to its doors in the mid-1800s, Dresden was quite content with its transportation situation.

In 1815 Gerald Lindsley, the area's first settler, made his way up the Sydenham River in a schooner named the *Olive Branch*. Many years later, a familiar sight at the Dresden dock was the *City of Dresden*, a fairly large steamboat. The late Mrs. Spearman (mother of Don Spearman, retired editor of Dresden's newspaper) enjoyed recalling popular steamboat excursions which ran during the summer between Dresden and Sarnia. These gala daylong trips included dinner and dancing—all for just fifty cents!

For almost thirty years stagecoaches met the Great Western trains at either Thamesville or Chatham to pick up mail for Dresden residents.

But in 1883 the Erie & Huron Railway was given a hearty welcome when its line was brought through Dresden. The town's population and economy showed immediate growth. This 87-mile railroad, with its southern terminus in the village of Erieau on Lake Erie, served mainly as a lumber line connection between Lake Erie and Sarnia, on Lake Huron. The Erie & Huron Railway was purchased by the powerful firm of Hiram Walker, who changed the line's name to Lake Erie & Detroit River Railroad. In 1902 this company was bought out by the Pere Marquette Railway, and after a short period of ownership was taken over by the Chesapeake & Ohio Railroad, better known as the "Chessie System."

Coach seats on the Erie & Huron were straw-covered in summertime. The straw was replaced with red plush during the winter months—though not the soft "plush" we know today. This scratchy material seemed to be made up of tiny barbs which worked their way through the stoutest of clothing. Coal stoves heated the old wooden coaches, and the coal-oil lamp that swung from the ceiling gave off a pale, eerie light.

The Erie & Huron was strictly a workhorse railway whose aspirations did not include competition with either the Great Western or Grand Trunk railways. Dresdenites nicknamed one of the company's two steam locomotives "Jack the Ripper," after a notorious British murderer of that era, and the other "John the Baptist," because it had to stop at every station for water. They had nicknames for the railway companies too—always uncomplimentary. Trains on the Erie & Huron were usually late, and the company suffered financial difficulties. For these reasons the company's initials had come to stand for "easygoing and hungry."

For the sake of the economy, the stations built for the Erie & Huron Railroad were constructed of wood. The grey, drab station at Blenheim became quite a showplace when ruby-red glass was placed in the small upper panes of the station's windows.

The exterior of the compact little station in Dresden was painted an appropriate Dresden blue. The wooden trim surrounding the windows and doors, the amusing little gable rising above the front entrance, and the notched edging of the roof were painted white.

Before the days of automobiles, passengers were picked up at the station by the town "bus," drawn by a team of two horses. Another horse-drawn wagon carried luggage and freight into town.

Dresden no longer has railway passenger service, but the little frame station has been preserved as one of the attractions at a neighbouring pioneer village.

The exterior of the compact Dresden station was painted an appropriate Dresden blue with white trim. Before the days of automobiles, train passengers were picked up by the town "bus," which was drawn by a team of horses. This image is from a period postcard.
Don Spearman collection

The Great Western Railway station at Ethel was demolished over twenty years ago. A single rusting track is all that remains of the former rail line that once brought excitement and prosperity to Ethel.

ETHEL

When the rumour began to spread that a railway was being built through the Queen's bush in Huron County, every little hamlet in the area visualized itself becoming a great metropolis! Ethel, a tiny settlement east of Brussels, was no exception.

In a letter to the editor of the Seaforth newspaper in 1869, the Ethel news correspondent wrote, "Our little village and surrounding vicinity is in a furor of excitement over the railway question. Judging from the speeches and discussions you hear going on in almost every hole and corner, we shall have a locomotive from some part of the world (I cannot tell you from where) puffing over our sacred soil before another year is past. Hoping that such may be the case, and that there will be a big station at Ethel, is the wish of your correspondent."

The correspondent surely must have been disappointed when the tracks of the Wellington, Grey & Bruce Railway were not laid along Main Street. In fact, the tracks were laid a half mile south, at a four corners known as Tyndell, and the sign painter spelled the station name "Eethel"—yet another annoyance to the village. (The sign was eventually corrected.)

Although the tracks were laid in 1873, it was another year before the first work train appeared. The same newspaper correspondent reported the event, saying, "On Friday last we were treated to the sound of a whistle of a passing train. It is supposed that the road will be opened for regular traffic to Kincardine soon, and the sooner the better, as there is a large quantity of square timber already delivered at the track, ready to be shipped to Quebec as soon as the road is open." But the wait continued.

In September 1874 a group of irate men from the district appointed delegates to press the WG&B's directors for the opening of the railroad. The delegates threatened to commence legal proceedings at once if no action was taken.

Telegrams that arrived in November were worded to the effect that the line would be opened by December 1st. On December 11th the district delegates were notified that the Wellington, Grey & Bruce Railroad had been taken over by the more prosperous Great Western Railway, and the public was assured that "the people will be well repaid for the long delay in the opening of the railroad."

A week before Christmas an excursion train treated everyone along the line to a free trip to Kincardine. A real holiday spirit spread through the coaches, and no one complained about the shortage of seats.

Another newspaper correspondent wrote about his village being in "quite a state of excitement on account of trains having commenced to run. Some of us expect to be rich in a few days, and our troubles will be over."

At last, Ethel had train service! But severe winter storms in 1874 and '75 created constant delays. In February of 1874, twenty-foot snowdrifts halted all trains for almost three weeks. The conductor on one train buried beneath drifts near Ethel went from house to house in the village, collecting baskets of food for his stranded passengers.

Business was brisk at the Ethel station in 1877. Four passenger trains and two mixed trains stopped at the station every day except Sunday. Mail was dropped off in bags and taken up to the village post office by John Johnson. Ab Sanders's express dray met all the trains, and half of his horse-drawn conveyance served as a taxi for train passengers. William Angus, who shipped his cheese to the city, reported that the total cost of cheese production in 1887 amounted to slightly over two cents per pound (including shipping expenses)! Other shippers were William Spende, an earthenware manufacturer, and John Cober, who built carriages and windmills. These old industries have long since vanished.

The Great Western Railway built a three-storey hotel next to the railway station. It had seven bedrooms, a dining room and a popular bar that was well patronized by the travelling salesmen who stayed at the hotel.

One unforgettable occasion at the hotel was the "Night of the Big Hunt." Two teams of men, twelve on each team, staged a daylong squirrel hunt. Shouldering their muzzleloaders, they headed for the woods. At sunset the hunters met at the hotel to tally their scores. It has never been established whether the staggering total of squirrel tails was arrived at before or after the jolly celebration that night. One team claimed to have bagged 3,900 squirrels, and the other team claimed 3,002. Ethel's squirrel population must have been totally wiped out!

No trace of the Great Western Railway hotel can be found today, and the railway station was demolished over twenty years ago. Station operators employed at the Ethel railway station include George Knight from Exeter, a Mr. Gillies in 1890, Mr. Heyd in 1897, Mr. Mitchell and John Smith in 1899, and J. Scott 1903. James Murray and Percy Currie were also there in the early years of the century. Harry Walls was in charge at the time of the station's closing. Walls later became County Clerk in Woodstock.

A single rusting track is all that remains of the old railroad that stirred up so much excitement when it was built in 1873. The sadness of the scene is softened during the summer when clumps of colourful wildflowers grow in profusion.

CN 2-8-0 2724 digs out while on a snowplow assignment in the 1930s.
Ken Liddell collection

EXETER

A hundred-year-old gold spike may still hold down a rusting bit of track somewhere along the old London, Huron & Bruce Railroad, about thirty-one miles north of London.

It was on Christmas Day 1875 when LH&B crews working from north and south met at Exeter. The historic moment called for a special celebration, a traditional gold spike ceremony. For almost three years labourers had been cutting through Huron County's dense forests, bridging rivers and valleys on this seventy-four-mile railway. The customary financial embarrassments had plagued the company's directors, delaying construction. Over two hundred and twenty thousand dollars still had to be paid to the contractor before the line could be opened for traffic. But from then on, the LH&B was a great success.

Exeter had become an incorporated village in 1873, just three years prior to the arrival of the railway, but pioneers had been coming to the area gradually since the opening of the London–Goderich Road. Among the early Huron County pioneers were James Willis and his wife, Jane, who had emigrated from Ireland. When they took up their lot on the London Road survey, they became the first settlers in the area that is now Exeter. Wolves were still a nuisance at that time, and Jane Willis never forgot the terror she felt the day a wolf dashed through their cabin door and fled with a great roast of venison.

Jane Willis was still alive when the first passenger train steamed into Exeter. She must surely have compared the exciting event with her own footsore arrival in 1832. At the time, there was no transportation along the newly built roads. A few of the more fortunate pioneer families had carts and a team of oxen, but like the Willises, the majority came on foot.

The first mail service along the London–Goderich Road was handled by Isaac Rattenbury, who settled in Goderich in 1834. With the coming of the railway, mail was carried and sorted on special mail cars.

Privately owned stagecoach lines made their appearance in the late 1830s, providing a much-needed convenience but little comfort for travellers. Operators of these crude conveyances were notorious for their reckless driving and lust for liquor. For a mere fifty cents you could make the round trip from Exeter to London and back—if you had the courage to travel by stage.

In 1871 news spread through the country almost overnight when a group of London financiers announced their intention to build a railroad from London through central Huron County to Wingham. In 1874 an agreement was made between the directors of the London, Huron & Bruce and the Great Western Railway of Canada. The pioneer Great Western contracted to construct and lease the LH&B. (In 1882 the Great Western amalgamated with the Grand Trunk Railway.)

Settlers along the proposed line were impatient with the seemingly endless delays, but towards the end of 1875 references to the railway's progress were reported frequently in newspapers. The Seaforth paper published a list of the names of station agents appointed along the line and added a reassuring note, "We believe this line has secured an efficient staff of officers and persons whom the public will find courteous and obliging in all their dealings with them." Mr. W. Hayden was selected as Exeter's station agent. At Hensall there would be Mr. W. Dench; Charles Deane at Brucefield; and G.W. Rialton at Clinton.

The first freight train on the LH&B came to Exeter in early January and dropped off a large amount of freight for merchants from the surrounding villages.

On the morning of January 20, 1876, a special train left Wingham and headed south to London for the gala opening of the London, Huron & Bruce Railway. Coaches were filled with prominent men from every village along the line—Belgrave, Blyth, Londesborough, Clinton, Brucefield, Kippen, Hensall, Exeter, Clandeboye, Centralia,

There have been three stations in Exeter's history. The second station was
destroyed by a mysterious fire in 1911. The present station was built by the
Grand Trunk Railway soon after this catastrophe.

Denfield, Ilderton and Ettrick. This jovial trainload had a rousing six-hour head start on the ceremonies by the time their train pulled into London. However, the stirring musical greeting played by the 7th Battalion Band, and the salute of the artillery battery, revitalized their energy for the daylong celebration ahead.

All of London was decked out for the occasion. Flags, bunting and marching bands set the mood for the day. But the high spot of the agenda was the grand banquet prepared for over six hundred guests. Few men had ever sat down to such a feast! Speech after speech, interspersed with innumerable toasts, carried the affair far into the night. Eventually, the party broke up, with everyone satisfied that the London, Huron & Bruce Railway had been suitably launched.

Like most other communities along the line, Exeter enjoyed rapid growth and prosperity with the coming of the railway. Many hotels were built along the main street, and most sent private stagecoaches to meet each train. Probably the most popular hotel among salesmen and business travellers was the Exeter Station Hotel.

By February of the railway's first year, its passenger service had become so popular that an extra coach had to be placed on the regular train. Mail trains from the north arrived daily at 10:05 a.m., and the mixed train came in at 4.05 p.m. Trains from the south arrived at 10:30 a.m. and 6:35 p.m. And of course a great many freight trains plied the line as well.

Special trains were always a popular attraction at the station, especially the circus train with its gaily painted coaches! Touring performers, opera singers and theatrical troupes usually came during the fall and winter months, adding a bit of splendour to life in a quiet village.

Enthusiastic welcomes were also given to visiting politicians, who made a point of stopping at the important Exeter station. And when Sir Charles Tupper, Canada's sixth Prime Minister, visited in 1896, a parade with bands formed at the station to greet him.

The location of Exeter's railway station was not generally popular. Most people thought such an important building belonged on the main street instead of almost out of sight on the west side of the village. The tracks had been laid through property belonging to Isaac Carling, who had donated a large lot for the station.

There have been three stations in Exeter's history, plus a large frame water tower, stock pens and freight sheds. The second station was destroyed by a mysterious fire in 1911, and the present station was built by the Grand Trunk Railway soon after this catastrophe. Exeter residents were proud of this handsome new building.

Throughout its history, the London, Huron & Bruce Railway was always regarded affectionately as part of the family. Early morning trains were filled with chattering pupils going off to continuation school. Farmers and their wives caught up on all the gossip and local news while travelling down to the London market with crates of fowl and baskets of produce. It was the "Butter and Egg Special."

When passenger service came to an end in 1956, it was a sad day for almost everyone in Exeter. The station which once employed ten men, and whose revenue from passengers was almost seven thousand dollars in its first year, is now padlocked and boarded up, but many old-timers in town still remember the good old days of the LH&B Railway and dream of seeing some new use for their old station.

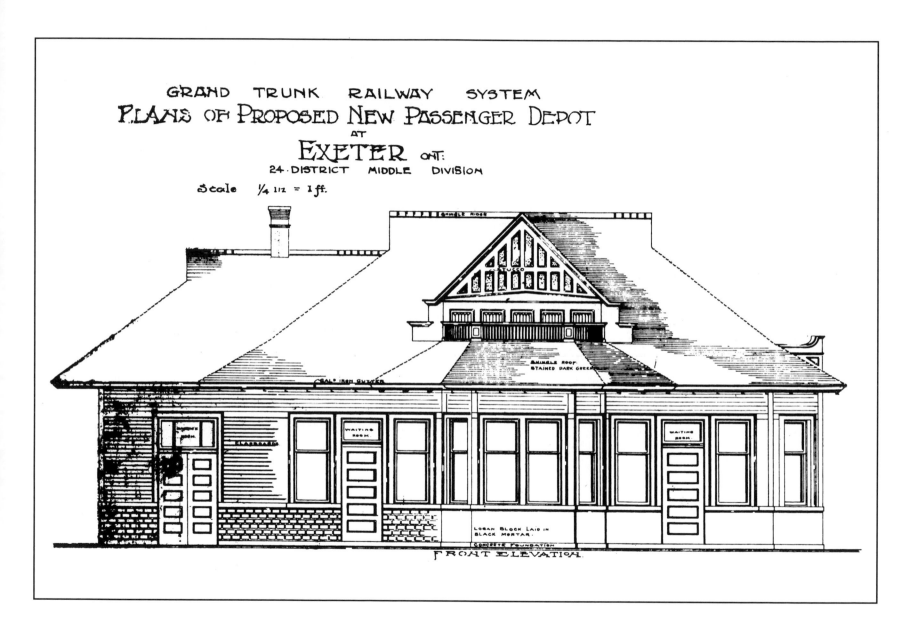

GRAND TRUNK RAILWAY SYSTEM
PLANS OF PROPOSED NEW PASSENGER DEPOT
AT
EXETER ONT:
24 DISTRICT MIDDLE DIVISION

Scale 1/4 112 = 1 ft.

FRONT ELEVATION

Plan drawings for the Grand Trunk
passenger depot at Exeter.

REAR ELEVATION

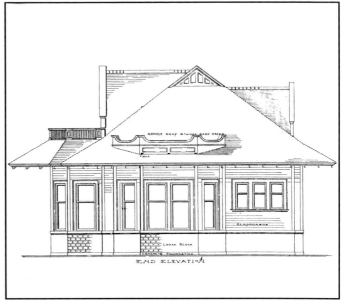

END ELEVATION

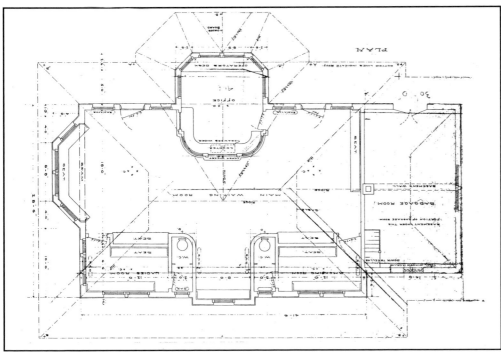

This photograph of the Flesherton CPR station was taken in 1970. In the 1930s and 40s, the CPR ran special weekend ski trains between Toronto and Flesherton.

FLESHERTON

If you were a teenager and a skiing enthusiast almost fifty years ago, Flesherton station will surely awaken marvellous memories of an era that ended too quickly.

Back in the 1930s and 40s, the Canadian Pacific Railway ran special ski trains from Toronto every Friday night from November until late March. Most of the passengers were headed for either Flesherton or Caledon, where the rolling hillsides were cushioned with deep, powdery drifts.

You needed a good sense of humour to survive those trips! The dusky, ancient CPR coaches offered very little comfort. They were either too hot or too cold. When your train arrived in Orangeville, you were given about ten minutes to rush into the station restaurant for coffee and pie. In another half hour you would be in Flesherton, where your host would be waiting with his big, open, horse-drawn sleigh. It is doubtful that any of us were then aware of the fascinating history of the railroad.

It was a narrow-gauge line built in 1871 by the Toronto, Grey & Bruce Railway. Its first locomotive, the *Caledon*, had two boilers and used wood for fuel. It took two firemen to keep the pressure up on these locomotives, which were built by Fairlie in England. They had no brakes and relied on the good judgement of the engineer when slowing for a station stop. Quite regularly the locomotive simply glided right past the station. This took place at the opening ceremony for one of the stations. The *Caledon* finally came to a stop inside the front window of a local business.

By the time the CPR leased the Toronto, Grey & Bruce in 1884, the narrow-gauge railway had been converted to standard gauge, with tracks spaced 4 feet 8 inches apart. It was the last railroad in Ontario to be converted.

The late Herbert Stitt, a CPR engineer on the Toronto – Owen Sound line, experienced some of the worst winter storms in Ontario's history. In the paralyzing storms of 1943 and 1947, entire trains were buried and six locomotives were required to push the snowplow through drifts as high as the tops of the telegraph poles!

As with all other railroads, the line built by the Toronto, Grey & Bruce had a few train wrecks in its history. Probably the worst was the Great Horseshoe Wreck, which took the lives of seven passengers (two from Flesherton) and injured 114. The Great Horseshoe Wreck happened on September 2, 1907, and involved a special train filled with passengers heading south for a day at the Toronto Exhibition. The infamous Horseshoe Curve near Caledon, along the Niagara Escarpment, had a 462-foot bend. Engineers had to use extreme caution in this area. Even after the investigation, no one was certain as to the cause of the accident. This section of track was removed in 1932, but its outline is still visible in a farmer's field.

When passenger service was discontinued along this historic railroad in 1970, most stations were closed and later destroyed or dismantled. The Orangeville station was moved to the centre of town, where it is now a restaurant.

It is still possible to see where the Flesherton station once stood (in Ceylon, a mile west of town). In its good years, it was well cared for by the station agent who lived with his family on the second floor. It was painted the traditional "railway red," and its waiting room was furnished with the usual uncomfortable wooden benches.

In the days when special ski trains were popular, each Sunday evening through the winter the waiting room of the Flesherton station was filled with weary skiers awaiting the arrival of the southbound train.

FOREST

In the early 1800s, choosing a name for a new settlement wasn't always easy. Often, the first settler in the area assumed that his surname would be chosen. Others, proud of their homeland, preferred to adopt the name of the village they had left behind. At milepost 159 on the Grand Trunk's newly laid line between St. Marys and Sarnia, engineers stopped their trains to refuel their wood-burning locomotives. As this was a heavily wooded area, the train crews simply called it "Forest." The name stuck. In 1861, two years after the arrival of the railway, the community applied for a post office and requested that it be registered with the name Forest.

The first passenger train arrived in Forest in 1859, the same year that the hamlet's first general store opened for business. A year later Forest's first railway station was built. It was a simple frame building surrounded by sheds, stock pens, a handcar house, and a large hand-pump-operated water tank for the steam locomotives. The drafty freight shed served as Forest's first church for a short time.

Forest had its share of dramatic episodes in the early days of the station. In 1896, when a pair of bank robbers plotted a way to blast open the safe at the town bank, they began at the railway station. The thieves stole enough wooden railway ties to surround the bank's safe. The sound of the exploding dynamite was so successfully muffled by the ties that not even the constable on duty heard the blast.

Another tense situation occurred at the station in 1888 when Forest was seeking town status. A population of two thousand was required to become a town. When it was discovered that an immediate population increase was needed, the quick thinking of former reeve Albin Rawlings saved the day. A passenger train standing at the station was detained for an hour while every passenger and crew member was registered as a citizen of Forest! Albin Rawlings was unanimously voted in as first mayor of the newly incorporated town.

After Forest's first railway station was destroyed by fire in 1898, plans were drawn for an elegant new station building, which opened in 1901. A circular waiting room was one of the attractive features of the new station. A separate waiting room was included for the comfort of the ladies, and above it was the turret room that was so popular in Grand Trunk Railway stations. Another small turret was placed over the telegraph operator's area, overlooking the tracks.

The Forest station always bustled with activity. Eight passenger trains came through every day, as well as long freight trains. For only two dollars and forty cents you could make a return trip to Toronto! But when the novelty of automobiles put new excitement into travelling, the popularity of passenger trains declined.

It was a sad occasion when the last passenger train made its final trip in 1956. The station continued to be used for freight service, but eventually it too was closed. A farmer bought it for just three hundred dollars and used it as a barn.

When towns lose their stations and railway tracks, as well as the familiar sound of train whistles, most of them soon forget. But the Forest Heritage Railway Association keeps memories alive with collections of railway memorabilia and a well-preserved old Grand Trunk caboose that serves as a tourist information centre during the summer.

In 1985 a unique public library was built on the site of the Grand Trunk Railway station. Using architects' drawings acquired from the National Archives, a modified replica of Forests' second station was created. Landscape gardeners surrounded the building with a lawn, evergreen trees, and a sunken garden with benches along its paths.

Although trains may never pass through Forest again, the town's railway memories live on, and no one could be more pleased with the town's station-library than railway historian John H.F. Hoyle and members of the Forest Heritage Railway Association.

Forest's first railway station was built in 1860. Its drafty freight shed served as
the town's first church for a short time.
R. Brown collection

Forest's second station, built by the Grand Trunk in 1901, eventually closed and was sold to a farmer for three hundred dollars. The town's public library is a replica of this station based on architects' drawings from the National Archives.

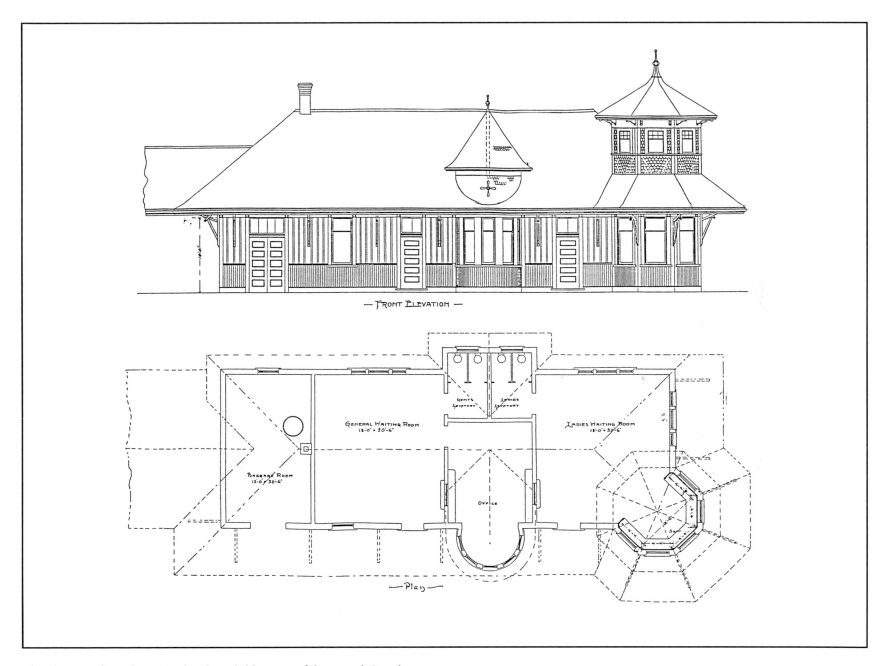

— FRONT ELEVATION —

— Plan —

GENERAL WAITING ROOM
13'-0" × 20'-6"

LADIES WAITING ROOM
13'-0" × 20'-6"

BAGGAGE ROOM
13'-0" × 20'-6"

GENTS
LAVATORY

LADIES
LAVATORY

OFFICE

Plan drawings from the original architect's blueprint of the second Grand
Trunk station at Forest.

This handsome brick station replaced Ingersoll's original frame station. The
first passenger train to stop in Ingersoll arrived on December 15, 1853.

INGERSOLL

Ingersoll's railway history began on December 15, 1853, when the first Great Western Railway passenger train stopped in town. Almost everyone was there for this exciting occasion. While the train was taking on wood and water for the steam locomotive, bottles of champagne appeared and toasts were proposed to the success of the Great Western.

On January 27, 1854, regular passenger service began, and it became possible to travel to Windsor in just a few hours! But 1854 was a black year for the Great Western. It was remembered as "the year of the accidents," as seventeen wrecks claimed many lives.

The first railway station, an unimaginative frame building, was eventually replaced by the handsome brick station that stands today. It has been painted a warm shade of grey, with white trim around the windows and the steep gable roof.

When the Credit Valley Railway completed a line from Toronto to St. Thomas in 1881, it went ahead with plans to continue the line up through Woodstock and Ingersoll in Oxford County. Their tracks ran parallel to the Great Western's. In 1882 the Great Western Railway amalgamated with the more prosperous Grand Trunk Railway. On November 9, 1883, the Credit Valley Railway amalgamated with the CPR.

Without doubt, the most ambitious railway to arrive in Ingersoll was the Tillsonburg, Lake Erie & Pacific Railway, which actually started at Port Burwell on Lake Erie. The first section of this railway was opened in 1896, and the line's maiden trip was best forgotten. Crowds gathered to watch the train leave and were stunned when the locomotive slid off the track and sank into a quagmire. After eleven long years of labour, the tracks finally reached Ingersoll. But the company was soon taken over by the CPR and all hopes of reaching the Pacific were abandoned.

The most exciting trains to watch passing through Ingersoll were the famous silk trains, whose precious cargo contained bales of cocoons bearing live silkworms. Their value was in the millions of dollars! The fastest ships in the world carried this cargo from Japan to Vancouver. Trains waiting at the harbour were loaded at a rate of 470 bales in just eight minutes. Speed of delivery was so essential that the New York-bound trains carrying this fragile cargo were given the right of way on their entire journey across Canada. Powerful steam locomotives could make the trip in just seventy-four hours and fifty minutes, at an average of fifty-five miles an hour. The longest silk train on record carried twenty-one cars, with a cargo valued at seven million dollars! The Depression years and the introduction of synthetic materials ended the silk-train era.

The Woodstock, Thames Valley, Ingersoll Electric Railway operated between Ingersoll and Woodstock from 1901 until 1925. Its rolling stock included a quaint "toonerville trolley" called *Estelle*. The motorman could stand on a platform and operate the car from either end. Sixteen people could sit along the two benches, and a potbelly stove in the corner kept them warm in winter.

A second coach was added to the line with the purchase of an open-air car named the *City of Woodstock*. This coach was used only in summertime and was always filled with picnickers. Motormen had one scheduled stop to make, at Beachville, but could be persuaded to stop anywhere along the line. The popularity of automobiles and the economic toll of the Depression brought a sad end to this toonerville trolley service which had provided a quarter of a century of good fun.

Front Elevation

This architect's rendering of the proposed Grand Trunk station at Ingersoll
was done by R. Armour for chief engineer John Hobson and dated November
30, 1885.

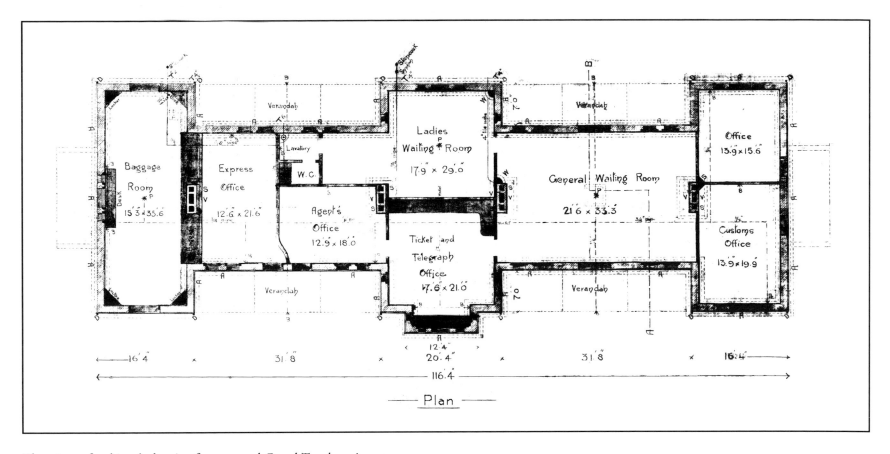

Baggage Room *P 15'3 × 35.6

Express Office 12'6 × 21'6"

Agent's Office 12'9 × 18'0

Lavatory

W.C.

Verandah

Ladies Waiting * Room P 17'9" × 29'0"

Ticket and Telegraph Office 17'6" × 21'0"

General Waiting Room * 21'6 × 33'3

Office 13'9 × 15'6

Customs Office 13'9 × 19'9

Verandah

Verandah

Verandah

16'4" 31'8" 12'4" 20'4" 31'8" 16'4"

116'4"

— Plan —

Plan views of architect's drawing for proposed Grand Trunk station at Ingersoll.

The Listowel Grand Trunk station was built on land where the village's first settlers, the Binningses, once lived. When passenger service ended, the station became a recreation centre. This photo was taken in 1970.

LISTOWEL

In the late 1800s Ontario maps looked like enormous spider webs, with dozens of railway lines crisscrossing in all directions. Most were built by ambitious small companies who had very little financial backing. Inevitably, these companies were absorbed by the powerful Great Western, Grand Trunk, or Canadian Pacific. The Port Dover & Lake Huron Railway was one such company.

The Port Dover & Lake Huron reached Listowel with great relief in 1877. How demoralizing it must have been for company officials when the only locomotives they could afford were those from the scrap heap of an American firm. But General Superintendent A.G. Atwater believed in making the most of any material that could be bought cheaply. The railway's two locomotives were called #1 and the *Black Crook* —and only one engineer was ever able to coax the latter to run! Engineer Bob McNabb would tighten up the *Black Crook's* leaky flues with bran the night before he had to take the locomotive out. He also kept an ample supply of baling wire to reinforce any loose running gear. It was fortunate indeed when the ailing Port Dover & Lake Huron Railway was absorbed by the Grand Trunk!

Cattle day was a weekly event at the Grand Trunk yards. Drovers delivered the animals to the railway pens early in the day, then spent a social hour drinking ale and chatting with other farmers at the railway hotel.

The Grand Trunk station in Listowel was built on land where the village's first settler lived. John Binnings and his wife and child had loaded their possessions into a wagon in Hamilton and made the long trek up to the Queen's bush country in 1851. An abandoned shack became the Binnings' home, and it was seven years before they saw another living soul! This unexpected visitor was "Henry," from whom John Binnings bought two hundred acres, some of which he later sold to the Grand Trunk.

The passenger station built on the Binningses' property in Listowel became a successful recreation centre in the community when passenger service was discontinued more than twenty years ago.

The Canadian Pacific Railway built a branch line from Listowel to Linwood in 1908. Four mixed trains shuttled back and forth daily until 1939. Linwood was the junction with the main CPR line.

Mixed trains are now a thing of the past. Very few people can remember them. They consisted of freight cars, cattle cars, flatcars and one passenger coach, which often served as an office on wheels for travelling salesmen. Passenger coaches were often embalmed with the mixed aroma of cigar smoke and orange peel.

When the first CPR train arrived in Listowel in 1908, Joseph Fair was the engineer. Fair had been an employee with the Canadian Pacific Railway since 1885. When the last run was made out of Listowel on May 13, 1939, Joe Fair was once again at the throttle. He wore new overalls and cap for the occasion, and this popular elderly gentleman was given a tremendous ovation as he climbed up into the cab.

Sentimental passengers filled the day-coach for the final trip. Railway officials attended, as well as retired railway men who had worked with Fair and with John Livingstone, the station agent who sold the first passenger ticket in the CPR Listowel station.

The late Herbert Stitt, retired CPR engineer who died in June 1992, served as Joe Fair's fireman in the days of coal-burning locomotives. Engine 7048 was their pride and joy. All the brass and copper fittings shone like gold from years of constant polishing by the crews. It was said that no Royal train was ever as pampered.

In his book, *I Remember,* Herbert Stitt stated that the CPR's annual receipts from this short branch line amounted to over seventy-five thousand dollars annually. He also described the relentless winter storms. Drifts on the tracks sometimes reached twenty feet high. A bad

This postcard of the Listowel CPR station is date-stamped December 31, 1908.

storm could cut off Listowel from the outside world for three days. Snowplows and additional locomotives were useless.

Many memories were made on the Listowel CPR subdivision. When retired railway men get together, their conversations still begin, "Oh, I remember the winter of...."

This timetable from 1920 shows train schedules for the Listowel sub-division between Listowel and Linwood.

Retired engineer Joseph Fair returns to the throttle on May 13, 1939, for the CPR's last run out of Listowel. Also pictured are fireman Bill Morrison (in overalls) and watchman Charles Wambole.

WESTBOUND TRAINS INFERIOR DIRECTION			Miles from Linwood	Telegraph Office	LISTOWEL SUBDIVISION	Telegraph Calls	EASTBOUND TRAINS SUPERIOR DIRECTION		
SECOND CLASS							SECOND CLASS		
	653 Mixed l Daily ex. Sun.	651 Mixed l Daily ex. Sun.			STATIONS		652 Mixed a Daily ex. Sun.	654 Mixed a Daily ex. Sun.	
	P.M.	A.M.					A.M.	P.M.	
....	8.15	10.55	.0	D	.........LINWOOD.......YKW	W O	7.40	3.05	....
					4.4				
....	f 8.27	f 11.10	4.4	....	.........DORKING.........	....	f 7.28	f 2.50	....
					4.7				
....	f 8.40	f 11.25	9.1	....	.........TRALEE.........	....	f 7.15	f 2.35	....
					7.1				
....	8 55	11.45	16.2	D	.........LISTOWEL.......KCW	S R	7.00	2.15	....
	P.M.	A.M.					A.M.	P.M.	
	a Daily ex. Sun. 653	a Daily ex. Sun. 651					l Daily ex. Sun. 652	l Daily ex. Sun. 654	

Railway Crossing at Grade with Grand Trunk Factory Siding just north of station in Listowel Yard, not interlocked.

Maintenance of way employees will provide unattended flag protection as per rules 51 and 52 on page 18 maintenance of way rules and instructions.

LUCKNOW

The methods used to attract customers to modern real estate subdivisions are often garish, but a unique attention-getter used to bring land buyers to the Queen's bush in Bruce County in 1853 makes today's promoters look like novices.

In the area which would become Lucknow, lots were sold by auction in virgin forests where white men had never set foot previously. A mammoth explosion echoed through the countryside on sale day, scattering shocked potential buyers in all directions. It was later revealed that gunpowder had been packed in holes in twenty-one trees and ignited. The dazed crowd stayed on, bought property, and the village of Lucknow was born. By 1880 the village's population had swelled to fifteen hundred. There were mills, carriage factories, liveries, eight hotels, churches, and a daily stage linking Lucknow with Walkerton and Goderich.

Lucknow became an important shipping centre after the Wellington, Grey & Bruce Railway built its line through town in 1873. At train time the station platform was usually covered with cases of eggs, milk cans and crates of complaining chickens. A tremendous amount of grain was also shipped from Lucknow.

Lucknow was on the southern extension of the Wellington, Grey & Bruce Railway and was leased by the Great Western Railway in 1874. Its chief competitor, the Grand Trunk Railway, took over the operation in 1893 when Great Western experienced financial difficulty.

While Lucknow was still rejoicing over its good fortune in becoming a railway town, the community experienced its first scandal. A man from Harriston who adopted the alias of "Peter Hammer" had left his wife and come to Lucknow to live. He became enamoured with the hired girl at his boarding house, and soon there were rumours that the couple planned to elope. In a newspaper editorial, Hammer was called a "wily scoundrel." Despite a vigil kept by the men of Lucknow, the couple slipped out of town by train and disappeared. A warning to Peter Hammer was published in the newspaper, saying that he would be tarred and feathered if he ever returned.

The railway station was of single-storey frame construction with a spacious area for freight and express. A small house was provided for the track foreman and his wife, and a hotel was built by the Great Western.

Joe Conley, with his dray and horse, was a familiar sight at the station. He held the job of expressman and worked well into his eighties. As a cautious driver of horses, Conley was one of the best. But when he got his first and only car, he was said to be the most dangerous driver in Lucknow!

The late Garnet Henderson was Lucknow's last station agent. He came to town in 1952 and was there when the station closed in 1968. His wife, Evelyn, remembers the large waiting room with its green walls liberally covered with travel posters. A square box-stove kept the station comfortable during the winter.

Garnet Henderson didn't believe in locking the station door at any time. On cold nights, transients who could not afford to stay in hotels would stretch out on a bench in the waiting room. The privilege was never abused and vandalism was unknown.

The citizens of Lucknow were fortunate to have Garnet Henderson in their midst. For many years he coached baseball and hockey teams in town. His son Paul won international fame in hockey in 1972 when he helped win the Canada Cup for his team by scoring the winning goal in the last thirty-four seconds of the final game of the Canada-Russia series.

Bruce MacKenzie, the track foreman in Lucknow from 1947 until 1968, remembers his losing battles with the severe snowstorms that blew in off Lake Huron. As fast as he could clear out the switches,

In its heyday, Lucknow's station platform was routinely covered with cases of
eggs, milk cans and crates of complaining chickens awaiting their ride to market. When the station closed, the building was sold for its lumber.

snow filled them in again. During one of the worst winters on record, the MacKenzies kept several schoolchildren in their home for almost a week when a sudden storm paralyzed the town and made the surrounding country roads impassable.

Station agents who served in the Lucknow station were Mr. G. Hogart, James Henderson, Mr. Baird, Dan Hayes, R. Lowrie, Harvey Ham, F. Phillips, O. Martin, Alex Hamilton and Garnet Henderson.

Several months after the station closed, the building was bought for its lumber. The line remained in use for freight traffic until 1986, but in that year, the tracks were lifted. All that is left standing on the station property is the old red outhouse that they forgot to demolish.

This 1893 Grand Trunk Railway poster advertises a ticket sale for the August civic holiday.

MITCHELL

For railway buffs and photographers, the search for traces of the good old days of railroading is never-ending. These enthusiasts often find themselves exploring abandoned lines where the only action is killdeers building their nests between the ties. Many of these train buffs already have a trunkload of caboose photographs, but they can't resist the opportunity to snap just one more!

Generations of train-lovers in Mitchell have been lured to the overpass of the old Buffalo & Lake Huron Railway, about thirteen miles west of Stratford. In the days of steam locomotives, you could stand on the overpass from 6:10 a.m. until after dark, watching a daily procession of trains from east and west—freight trains, the express, mail trains.

The Buffalo & Lake Huron Railway was opened through Mitchell in 1858. The village prospered, and Mitchell became an incorporated town in 1873. The Grand Trunk Railway took over the B&LH in 1875. Mitchell saw its last passenger train in 1970, after 112 years of passenger service.

The view from the overpass remains dramatic, despite all the changes. Much of the old atmosphere is still there. The siding, which was always filled with cattle cars and grain hoppers, is still used, and the grain elevators are busy. Livestock was shipped out several times each week from the old stockyards, and on those days, roads leading into town were crowded with farmers' wagons hauling cattle for shipment. Across from the stockyards, on the north side of Georgina Street, a railway hotel was built for the convenience of travellers. It too has gone, but Chapman's Chopping Mill remains.

Mitchell's first railway station was a simple frame building with a heavy overhanging roof to protect passengers from the weather. Great stacks of cordwood were piled at one end of the station, in readiness for the wood-burning locomotives of that time. The historic *Toronto* was one of these locomotives. It was built in Toronto by James Good. History was made in 1853 when it pulled the first passenger train of the Ontario, Simcoe & Huron Union Railway from Toronto to Aurora.

Everyone in town was pleased with Mitchell's second railway station. More thought seemed to have been given to its design. The station's wooden-plank platform was always popular with small boys, who scrambled beneath the boards, hunting for coins that had slipped out of passengers' hands. Fire destroyed this station in 1914, and until a new one could be built, business was carried on in a Grand Trunk Railway coach.

Passenger trains had frequent scheduled stops at Mitchell in 1886. Travellers bound for Goderich had three choices. A timetable hung on the front of the station showed that the first train of the day left at 7:25 a.m. You could also leave at 1 p.m. or at 8:30 p.m. If you were travelling to Stratford to catch a Toronto train, you had your choice of leaving at 8:10 a.m., 2:40 p.m. or 6:10 p.m.

Large posters in the waiting room advertised holiday excursions sponsored by the Grand Trunk Railway. These trips were always low-priced and extremely popular. On Dominion Day 1877, the Holiday Special left Mitchell at for Toronto at 8:10 a.m. At Toronto passengers hustled down to the docks and boarded the splendid steamer *Empress of India*, which took them to see Lake Ontario. A Canada Southern train then took them to see Niagara Falls and over the bridge for a glimpse of the U.S. On the return trip, they came through Brantford, on to Stratford, and home. All for just two dollars and fifty cents!

Mitchell's third and last station served the community for over half a century. When it closed in 1970, station agent Laverne Jones was there to see it boarded up and padlocked. Among the other station agents who served at Mitchell's stations were John Dore, Alf Abray, Laurie Chapin, Maurice Hewitt, Charlie Oser and Stewart Kelly.

This station, Mitchell's third, closed in 1970, the year the town saw its last passenger train after 112 years of regular service.

Stewart Kelly of Appin first came to Mitchell in 1959. Following his retirement from the Goderich station in 1965, he returned to Mitchell to live. On his first night in Mitchell he decided to sleep in the station waiting room, as no arrangement had been made for accommodation. The lumpy, narrow cot from the baggage room just wasn't built for this lean six-foot-four man. Around midnight he was startled from his sleep by a flashlight shining through the window onto his face. The beam slowly traced the length of his body, then an astounded policeman said, "That's the longest man I've ever seen!"

Like many other railway men, Stewart Kelly had always known railway life. He was fascinated by all the sounds and smells of the trains. As a boy, after school he would drop into the Appin station for a chat and game of checkers with Mr. Strode, the station agent. Under Mr. Strode's tutorage, he mastered the telegrapher's key and learned how to run a railway station. In 1941 he was employed by Canadian National Railways. He still recalls his trepidation when he was put in charge of Appin's station. He claims he "shook like a leaf" while carrying out his first order to hold train #83 on the siding until train #16 from the east had come and gone.

The lovely old Grand Trunk Railway Park just east of the station in Mitchell was still there in Stewart Kelly's time, but a few great willows standing by the steps leading up to the station are all that remain of the park today. It was always an old-fashioned park and was popular with passengers waiting for trains. Summer concerts were held at the bandstand, and a canon from some long-forgotten battle always intrigued small boys.

There are still a few people in Mitchell who can remember the horse-drawn omnibuses from Hicks' House Hotel that came down to the station to meet every train. This service lasted for over sixty years. The stables and horses are gone, but Hicks' House Hotel, built by William Hicks, the founder of Mitchell, is a landmark on the main street. Hicks' House is believed to be the oldest business in continuous operation in all of Perth County.

Long ago, young couples used to stroll down to the railway park in the evening or sit on the platform bench and watch to see who would arrive on the late train. Young boys spent every Saturday at the station, hoping to get a ride with the engineer. Many people came down just to talk to the station agent. When the last passenger train pulled out on October 31, 1970, only a small, quiet group watched its departure. A memorable era had come to an end.

Engineers on the Goderich & Exeter Railway freight trains carry on the tradition of waving to rail buffs at the Mitchell overpass.

RENFREW

From the day it opened in 1896, everyone predicted that the CPR station in Renfrew would be there forever. The stonemasons from Scotland who built the station certainly intended it to last forever. But eighty-five years later a wrecking crew arrived. It was not easy to level the forty-by-ninety-foot granite-and-sandstone building. Watching the demolition of this historic landmark, Renfrew residents were deeply saddened.

There were two waiting rooms in the Renfrew station: one for the quiet enjoyment of ladies, and the other for the general public. A ticket office separated the waiting rooms, and a large room at the east end housed the express wagons, freight and baggage. During the days of steam locomotives, a large, stone-based water tower stood by the tracks just east of the station. Further along was the tall, spindly coal chute. (Locomotives taking on coal and water always had an audience.) There was a telegraph operator on duty at all times, and the clicking of the telegraph keys could always be heard. It was a mysterious sound; one you wished you understood.

In 1895, while the Renfrew station was being built, Sir William Van Horne's private train arrived in town. Van Horne had the engineer stop so that he could examine the work being done. He disapproved of the height of the station and ordered the rafters to be raised by another five feet. Sir William was then vice-president of Canadian Pacific. He had been knighted by Queen Victoria in 1894 for distinguished public services and in particular for his role in promoting the railways.

The Canada Central Railway built the first line into Renfrew in March 1873. It ran from Ottawa to Sand Point, on to Renfrew, and terminated at Callandar, just below North Bay. Canadian Pacific purchased this line in June 1881.

On December 29, 1884, the Kingston & Pembroke Railway opened for passenger traffic in Pembroke. Like most other railroads at that time, it had its nicknames. The K&P was sometimes referred to as the "Kick and Push." The company had twenty-four stations along its 103 miles of track.

In the early days, special trains could be scheduled for almost any occasion. Hockey teams and their fans filled the coaches for out-of-town games, and the train crews stayed to take them home. The famous Renfrew Millionaires hockey team had its own private railway coach!

The late Harry Hinchley, well-known historian and writer, recalled the story of two clergymen in Renfrew who set out together to attend a church conference in Smiths Falls. While chatting and laughing as they filled time in the Renfrew station waiting room, they missed the arrival and departure of their train! A local train on the K&P took them to Sharbot Lake, where they stopped at the hotel for noon dinner, then boarded still another train, which got them to Smiths Falls in time for the banquet which brought the conference to a close!

It was a sad day for Renfrew when passenger service to Kingston was discontinued in the 1960s. Eventually the tracks were removed and most stations were dismantled. One station still stands in Kingston, just across from the city hall. There is true elegance in its design, with mansard roof and magnificent stained-glass windows. It now serves as a tourist bureau.

Although both the CPR and CNR stations at Renfrew are no longer standing, freight trains still use these lines, and the VIA Transcontinental passes through regularly.

This wonderful granite-and-sandstone station at Renfrew opened for business
in 1896. It was demolished eighty-five years later—with much difficulty.

Renfrew Junction.
Public Archives photo 94781

This 4-4-0 Boyd Caldwell locomotive ran on the Kingston & Pembroke Railway, which opened for passenger traffic on December 29, 1884. The K&P was sometimes referred to as the "Kick & Push."
Public Archives photo C-53174

ST. THOMAS

Train travel was in its heyday when the Canada Southern Railroad built this fine red-brick station in 1873. It has always been called the "Grand Old Lady," a name it still bears proudly.

Back in the 1870s at least thirty passenger trains arrived in St. Thomas every day, as well as many freight trains. Day and night, the sound of chuffing yard engines, hooting steam whistles, ringing bells, and the constant pall of sooty coal smoke contributed to the exciting atmosphere of this busy rail centre.

Unfortunately, the identity of the architect of St. Thomas's historic station is unknown, though his signed drawings may still be filed away somewhere. Early photographs of the building show seven chimneys across the rooftop and a platform canopy for protection from snow and rain. During alterations these were removed, but the station otherwise retains its original design. The distressing changes are the absence of passengers and passenger trains. That era ended in 1979.

When the Michigan Central leased the line in 1880, the station became the company's head office. The upper floor was filled with well-lit offices, and on the ground floor were the waiting rooms, ticket office, baggage rooms and a large restaurant, which was a boon to passengers. Most trains stopped just long enough for a hungry traveller to dash inside and bring his sandwich back to the train. Some of the first-class trains allowed twenty-five minutes for passengers to relax and enjoy the fine catering of Captain Thomas Margetts, who managed the railway dining service.

The St. Thomas station was the place to find round-the-clock entertainment a century ago! You could watch great locomotives taking on coal and water, and over at the roundhouse and shops, where the company's 3,700 pieces of rolling stock were serviced, there was non-stop activity.

During the First World War, American troop trains en route to overseas embarkation points stopped at St. Thomas to give the men time to stretch their legs or sometimes to parade up the main street to the tempo of their own marching band.

On summer weekends the station platform was usually filled with crowds awaiting the special Niagara or Detroit excursion trains. It was always a big day when a theatrical train arrived, but most popular with everyone was the Barnum and Bailey circus train! Gaily painted circus cars lined up on sidings, and young boys crawled under fences to watch the animals being led down the ramp. There were cheers when Jumbo the famous elephant stepped through the doorway of his ornate, private "palace car."

St. Thomas became internationally known overnight following the Barnum and Bailey tragedy of September 15, 1885. All railway train crews had been ordered to wait for an all-clear signal that night before bringing trains into the yards. Unfortunately, one crew had not received the message.

After the evening's final performance, the circus animals were led down the track to their special cars. Jumbo and his companion elephant, Tom Thumb, were the last to leave the big tent. Suddenly, the trainer saw the headlight of an approaching locomotive on the line. Jumbo began to run and could not be persuaded to move to the safety of the ditch. Tom Thumb tried to catch up with his partner but was thrown into the ditch when the locomotive hit him. A moment later an agonizing roar was heard when Jumbo was struck. Fifteen minutes later he was pronounced dead. Circus-lovers around the world mourned his loss.

Barnum sued the railway for a hundred thousand dollars but settled for five thousand dollars plus free transportation for one year for his circus train. A century later, St. Thomas immortalized the famous circus elephant when they unveiled a larger-than-life-size statue of Jumbo.

The "Grand Old Lady" in St. Thomas covers an entire city block and was built for more than a quarter of a million dollars in 1873. In the 1870s at least thirty passenger trains arrived in St. Thomas every day.

Railway policeman employed at the St. Thomas station circa 1900.
Photographer unknown

The "Grand Old Lady" in St. Thomas covers an entire city block and was built for more than a quarter of a million dollars. Since 1873 it has been operated by Canada Southern, Michigan Central, the New York Central, and Amtrak. The building is presently owned by CN and CP Rail, who purchased the line from Conrail in 1985. It is to be hoped that this historic landmark will be preserved. Its stately design is unique in all Ontario railway architecture.

Walter A. Brown at Palmerston station, 1976. Brown was a conductor on a wayfreight running between Owen Sound and Stratford. The ornamental grillwork in the ticket office is typical of that used in many old stations.

SEAFORTH

Seaforth's first hundred years with the railway seemed to be constantly fraught with dissatisfaction. The town's first grievance was aired when the new railway opened for traffic in June 1858 and the station turned out to be just a flag stop. The building which eventually replaced it was regarded as a public eyesore.

Despite this, Seaforth began to prosper with the coming of the railway. But success brought its headaches, too. Seldom were there enough freight cars on hand to accommodate the huge quantities of salt, grain and produce waiting to be shipped. Grain dealers, who were losing money because of the situation, wrote testy letters to the Grand Trunk head offices in Montreal about the shortage of cars.

In one of his editorials in the Seaforth *Expositor* in 1874, the editor spoke bitterly about the Grand Trunk's shabby treatment of Seaforth: "The only thing about Seaforth that Seaforth people need feel ashamed of is the railway passenger station house. This public place is a ragged shanty. We do not know whether it will be of any use to again direct the attention of the Grand Trunk authorities to this public eyesore, but we do feel bound to say that it is a disgrace to the company and to the village. The building and grounds were made a gift to the company in the first place, and one would imagine that by this time they should be in the position to erect at least a respectable looking edifice. Besides being an eyesore, the present building is a dangerous nuisance. It is situated on one of the principal thoroughfares of the village, on which teams are constantly passing and repassing. There is scarcely a day that this street is not blocked by standing trains many times during business hours, impeding traffic and making it unsafe for travel. It is also almost a miracle that injury to life and limb is not occasioned by teams passing this place while trains are shunting around from one switch to another in front of this dilapidated building. Indeed, were it not for the praiseworthy vigilance of the station officials, accidents could scarcely be avoided almost daily."

In December 1869 Robert Baldwin Moodie was appointed station agent at the Grand Trunk station in Seaforth. His annual salary was six hundred dollars and his living quarters in the station were rent free. Moodie was the son of the famous author and early Canadian settler Susanna Strickland Moodie, whose book *Roughing It in the Bush* is still regarded as a classic among descriptive writings of the lives of Canada's early settlers.

While visiting her son and his family in Seaforth in May 1870, Susanna Moodie described in her letters to friends the crude living conditions at the railway station: "But oh such a droll little house. It is all on the ground floor, and the kitchen, parlour and two 8 by 6 bedrooms could all be contained in one tolerably sized room. Robert had to build a bedroom at his own cost for his wife's Mother and the two eldest little girls, ditto kitchen, for the old one neither kept out the rain, nor the snow, and was free to all the winds of heaven. I was domiciled in the state cabin, as I call the room in which I am writing to you in which I read and paint, think and pray, but I feel terribly cribbed, cabined and confined. The worst of it is that we have no privacy. The parlour door opening directly into the rail road which is only separated from us by a narrow board pavement, and trains are rushing to and fro all day shaking the wall and stunning our ears with the alarm. The house mistaken for the waiting room half the time, and as the two little bed closets open into the parlour my door is often opened by some strange person enquiring for 'the Station Master' and not long ago my daughter-in-law found a tipsy man in her room and had to go on to the platform to get some of the employees to get him out. All this is droll enough but it is annoying too."

In May 1876 the Huron *Expositor* mentioned a visit from Grand Trunk officials who were passing through to Goderich: "They took a

After twenty-five years of public complaint, Seaforth's citizens received a fine
new station in 1882. Susanna Moodie wrote of its predecessor, "Oh such a
droll little house...I feel terribly cribbed, cabined and confined."
Gordon Wright collection

look around the station house, but they did not attempt to wade through the almost bottomless quagmire at the rear of the elegant building. If they had, they would almost likely have sunk out of sight, and would never be visible above the earth."

However, there were some bright moments brought about by railway activities. On May 26, 1882, the "Big United States Circus" came for a three-day visit to Seaforth. It was reported that the special circus train was a mile long! Its coming was described as being filled with "triumphal grandeur." The two main attractions were the "Grand Racing Balloon Show" and the "Twenty Beautiful Lady Riders" who were "beautiful, daring, dashing and dazzling."

In the same year, the railway put on a special "Sabbath School excursion" train that took children to Goderich for the day. And in May, eighteen passenger cars were used to take holidayers on a "mammoth excursion" to the Falls.

The year 1882 was a banner one for the citizens of Seaforth. Not only were they treated to a circus and to excursion trips, but they were also given a fine new railway station! The wretched "eyesore" they had endured for twenty-five years was finally demolished. The editor of the Huron *Expositor* was well pleased when he described the attractive new station: "The erection of the new Grand Trunk Railway station house in the town is making satisfactory progress. The structure is 92 feet long by 24 feet in width, and will afford ample accommodation for the employees of the company at this point, as well as the travelling public. It is situated a few feet westward of the present building. At the east end will be the baggage room, next the gentlemen's waiting room, then the ticket office, and ladies' waiting room; while on the west end and upstairs will be the Agent's rooms. The workmanship is being done in the best and most substantial style by a staff of the company's own workmen. The building when completed will form a striking contrast to the present structure, which although well enough for its day is now altogether behind the age for the town of Seaforth and surrounding country in their present state of development."

Gradually, fewer passenger trains were needed on the line through Seaforth. Then came a decline in freight shipments. By 1965 Ben Williams, Seaforth's last appointed station agent, was the sole employee in this once busy station. There was no longer the need for an expressman, telegraph operator or someone to tend the freight shed. The stockyard and water tower had been dismantled many years ago.

Eventually, the railway station was demolished, bringing an unceremonious end to a building which was once so important to the town. A daily wayfreight belonging to the Goderich & Exeter Railway now passes through Seaforth. Times have changed.

This attractive brick-and-stone station at Stratford continues to be a pleasant reminder of the good old days. In 1870 the Grand Trunk began concentrating its workshops in Stratford and more than seven hundred families were moved to the area.

STRATFORD

Before the Grand Trunk Railway completed its line into Stratford, the hundred-mile trip to Toronto was one you had to plan carefully, then ask yourself, "Is this really necessary?" In 1855 a Stratford newspaper reporter was given an assignment in Toronto, and the trip took twenty-six hours! The reporter rode on a stagecoach to Kitchener, transferred to another one, which took him to Galt, where he caught a Great Western Railway train to Hamilton. There he hired a dray to take him to the harbour, where he was able to travel by boat to Toronto. It's fair to assume that the reporter was cheering when the first Grand Trunk locomotive arrived in Stratford on September 3, 1856, on a trial run.

Six weeks later, the railway was formally opened. Most people in town agreed that the occasion called for a celebration, but only a few offered to share the cost. One of Stratford's clergymen, who was opposed to a celebration, claimed that it would become just another excuse for "intemperance and carousing". He added that most people who attended these affairs only went to "imbibe in a good guzzle."

Despite the wrangling, the town made a favourable showing on the opening day. Stratford's Brass Band played "See the Conquering Hero Come." The flags flying in front of the railway station and the floral arches made an impressive setting for the arrival of railway officials and guests.

Reeve A.B. Orr gave an appropriate welcoming speech and assured his audience that the backwoods existence they had struggled with for twenty years was now a thing of the past. The guests were treated to a fine dinner followed by countless toasts and speeches.

Although the first passenger train in Stratford was brought in by the Grand Trunk Railway, the first railway tracks to enter the town were laid by the Buffalo, Brantford & Goderich Railway. However, this line was not in operation until 1858. The two companies came close to blows when the Grand Trunk track-laying crews tore up the Buffalo – Goderich tracks that lay in their path on the approach to Stratford. When General Manager Robert Barlow heard of this outrageous act, he wired back to his superintendent to tear up the offending GTR tracks and to put men on guard. When two flatcar loads of navvies from the GTR arrived on the scene, armed with pickaxes, tempers cooled and a peaceful settlement was worked out. However, the Buffalo company was insulted again when the Stratford newspaper allotted just a single paragraph to announce the official opening of the railway. No bands or cheering crowds greeted the first passenger train.

On October 7, 1875, a third railway company completed a line from Lake Erie to Stratford. This was the Port Dover & Lake Huron Railroad, which was later absorbed by Grand Trunk. The company built its own station at the corner of Nile and Falstaff streets. A fine parade and banquet were given in honour of this newcomer. The railway's two secondhand locomotives must surely have been an embarrassment to company directors. Their engine, the *Black Crook*, had been salvaged from a scrapyard and was said to be held together with baling wire!

Stratford had certainly become a true railway town. Lines stretched to Toronto in the east; to Sarnia in the west; to Wiarton and Owen Sound in the north; and to Simcoe and Port Dover in the south. There was also direct connection with Kitchener, Guelph, Listowel and Palmerston. In 1870 the Grand Trunk Railway began concentrating all its workshops in Stratford and more than seven hundred families were moved into the area. The local yards, with thirteen miles of sidings, were often filled. An average of three hundred cars were handled every twenty-four hours. In the shops there were pits for twenty-eight locomotives and an eighty-five-foot turntable. These shops covered an area of 313,020 square feet. In the early 1900s the company had its own fire and police departments at the Stratford yards.

A period postcard of the early
Grand Trunk station at Stratford.

After the Stratford railway station, the next most attractive Grand Trunk building was the three-hundred-foot-long greenhouse which provided plants for the beautification of station gardens throughout southern Ontario. Alf Williams, former head gardener at an English country estate, was in charge of the company's greenhouses, where he grew over eighty thousand plants for distribution. Stratford residents looked forward to Alf's annual fall horticultural exhibition.

As an incentive for station agents to beautify their station grounds, the Grand Trunk offered cash awards. One ambitious eastern Ontario station agent and his wife brought attention to their station with more than just attractive flower beds. On their lawns they built a fieldstone war memorial cairn and a horseshoe pitch. Window sills inside the station were filled with pots of red geraniums.

The Grand Trunk Railway operated its own pay car for station agents and track maintenance crews. This special train, usually hauled by well-known steam locomotive #505, was composed of only one coach, which served as a bank, office and living quarters for the paymaster, conductor and porter. Firearms were provided for the crew. This train travelled over all Grand Trunk lines in Ontario until 1902. Stratford station agents received seventy dollars per month in 1899, and telegraph operators, who worked twelve-hour shifts, received just fifty dollars.

Stratford's role as a busy railway town is over, and the locomotive shops and roundhouses which were the pride of the GTR are gone, but passenger trains from Toronto, bound for St. Marys, London and Sarnia, and long salt trains from Goderich, still pass through the yards. The attractive brick-and-stone station continues to be a pleasant reminder of yesterday, with its hanging baskets of flowers suspended from ornamental light standards along the platform and a Canadian flag flying above the building.

Commemorative plaque at Stratford's CN station.

STRATHROY

Back in the 1800s the coming of the railway frequently had the effect of a miraculous spring tonic on the growth of communities along its line. When the Great Western Railway of Canada completed a line through Strathroy in 1856, the town's lethargic pace changed almost overnight. It is believed that the entire population of four hundred came out to meet the first train. Five years later, their ranks would total over one thousand inhabitants.

The hamlet of Strathroy took shape around the river's edge, close to the mills, then spread out over the Sydenham flats. When railway surveyors became aware of the severe seasonal flooding in the area, they sought higher ground for their tracks. Loss of the railway would mean the sure demise of Strathroy, and influential residents eventually succeeded in persuading the railway to build just west of the settlement (after convincing John Frank that it would be to his advantage to have the railway run through his farmland).

Almost immediately Strathroy began to enjoy the benefits of being a railway community. Grain, sheep, cattle and lumber became its main exports. Farmers could ship grain by rail to Toronto in 1857 for just forty cents per barrel, or twelve cents per sixty-pound bushel bags. Squared timbers from the area's superb oak and walnut trees were in great demand in Quebec.

Strathroy's business section grew and improved shortly after the coming of the railway. The town soon had two doctors, carpenters, tinsmiths, wagonmakers, an agent for a trust and loan company, a newspaper owned by the well-known George Brown, and of course there was a well-stocked tavern.

Strathroy's first railway station was a fascinating place to linger. There was no lack of excitement on cattle-shipping day, when an almost endless parade of farmers' wagons lined up to unload their bawling cargo.

Whenever rural life seemed lackluster, reality could be left far behind by looking up at the colourful travel posters tacked on the waiting-room walls.

No one ever forgot the unique train that steamed out of Strathroy in 1887 carrying its fragile load! Bystanders held their breath as twenty-four freight cars were cautiously eased down the track past the station, each car carrying 10,500 dozen eggs. A total of 252,000 dozen eggs! You can imagine the locomotive engineer's sense of relief when he arrived at his destination that day after safely delivering his cargo.

Train accidents occurred frequently in the 1800s. The worst tragedy on the London to Sarnia line happened in 1874 and took the lives of several Strathroy residents. A lighted kerosene lamp fell and quickly set ablaze the wooden coach at the rear of the mixed train. Unfortunately, there was no communication cord to alert the engineer. The brakeman refused to make the perilous climb over the roofs of several petroleum cars and freight cars, but the conductor risked his life by scrambling across the top of the entire train. Nine people had perished in the gruesome accident by the time the train was brought to a stop.

A statistician attempted to alleviate train passengers' fears when they became alarmed by the frequency of train accidents. He claimed that more people died from falling out of windows than died on the railway.

Before the opening of the three-week-long Toronto Industrial Exhibition in September 1879, the railway published a special timetable with irresistibly reasonable rates. For just two dollars and fifty cents you could make the round trip between Strathroy and Toronto.

The low cost of building Strathroy's magnificent railway station is incredible in light of today's prices. This hundred-year-old station cost just nine thousand dollars when it was built in 1887. Public buildings at that time were built to last a lifetime and generally reflected residents' pride in the appearance of their community. Architects and

Strathroy's magnificent railway station was built in 1887 at a cost of just nine thousand dollars. Sixty-nine trains used to pass through Strathroy every day.

carpenters strived to create buildings which were sound and pleasing to the eye. One of the most outstanding embellishments of Strathroy's railway station is the attractive arrangement of wooden supports beneath the eaves.

It is still a pleasure to stand on the red-brick platform while waiting for the arrival of your train. The first locomotives on this line of the Great Western Railway were named after wild African animals—*Tiger, Elephant*, etc. Coaches were painted a cheerful canary yellow, as bright as the circus coaches which visited every year. The trains that come into the station today are still colourful. Amtrak cars are red, white and blue; cars run by VIA Rail are either blue and yellow or shades of grey, yellow and blue.

Sixty-nine trains used to pass through Strathroy every day. It is quieter at the station today, with eight passenger trains available daily, but everyone in this town of 7,800 people is grateful to still have their fine station.

A CPR wayfreight crew photographed at Orangeville station in 1972.

TORONTO

It's difficult to pinpoint the moment when the romance of railroading began to fade at Toronto Union Station and throughout the maze of tracks owned by Toronto Terminals Railway along the city's waterfront. Steam enthusiasts place the blame on the introduction of diesel locomotives and the gradual disappearance of steam engines with their inimitable haunting sounds.

Since 1854 the acres of track along Toronto's waterfront have been constantly alive with the sounds of trains. Small yard engines once fussed back and forth from track to track, hitching on or dropping off boxcars and coaches round the clock, making all manner of clanks, shrieks and groans. Diesel-hauled trains create little drama as they ease away effortlessly from a station. But when the great, powerful driving wheels of a steam locomotive went into motion, it was an exhilarating experience. Steam engines lived and breathed and could be creatures of many moods.

Train-watching was a popular form of entertainment before the Toronto railyards were drastically changed. The Bathurst Street bridge spanning the tracks was crowded with steam addicts on the weekends. Engineers usually let off an extra blast of sooty smoke when they passed under the bridge. No one objected to the clouds of cinders; pollution was unknown!

Scattered throughout the labyrinth of steel tracks in the railyards was an assortment of trackworkers' shanties, repair shops, signal towers, turntables, coal silos, water towers, switch lights, semiphores, faded red cabooses, and wooden coaches, all well seasoned with coal smoke. These landmarks and familiar sights gradually disappeared. Above their foundations rose the CN Tower, the tallest free-standing building in the world, and close by, the newly built Skydome. A wealth of artifacts were recovered by archaeologists in their final dig near the bases of these two new structures.

The Toronto Union Station and its massive yards are owned and operated by Toronto Terminals Railway Company, a wholly-owned subsidiary of Canadian National Railways and Canadian Pacific Limited, with each holding fifty percent of the stock.

Among the yards' less pretentious buildings were the squatty wooden gatehouses, such as the one which controlled traffic at the John Street level crossing. The gatekeepers' timing had to be perfect. The faded and peeling old gatehouses have since been removed, their services no longer required.

Everyone's favourite spot was Cabin D in the Bathurst Street yards. From its upper floor, operators manually controlled the smooth passage of trains. At one time there were 179 hand-operated switches and signal controls in Cabin D. The long bank of levers switched the tracks by a series of cables. Most operators required six months of supervised experience before they felt comfortable with their responsibility. A constantly boiling tea kettle on the back plate of a coal stove was one of the comforts in Cabin D. Many a good rabbit stew was prepared on the old stove back when rabbits still skittered around the Toronto yards.

In the 1980s, when it was announced that Cabin D would be demolished, Toronto decided to spend twenty thousand dollars to move and restore the historic building. One alderman who opposed the decision referred to the old cabin as a "glorified outhouse." It was surprising that he was not lynched by indignant railway enthusiasts! Retired CPR engineer Herbert Stitt was one who resented the remark. In his letter to the Toronto *Star*, he wrote, "Even as early as 1907, as a small boy, I have stood on the Bathurst Street Bridge and watched trains passing old Cabin D. 'Glorified outhouse' indeed! It certainly is not that to thousands of railroad men who through the years obeyed its signals, and still do! If that old Cabin D could talk, it could tell of the tragedies it witnessed over the years, because the Bathurst Street yards

Historic Cabin D at the Toronto Terminals Railway yards. Cabin D stood at
the west entrance to the downtown yards, under the Bathurst Street overpass.
Here, two CN subdivisions and a CP subdivision merged into the Front Street
trackage.

Gateman's tower at the Toronto Terminals Railway Strachan Avenue yards.

Crossing shanty at the Toronto Terminals Railway yards. This photograph was taken in 1968.

Looking east from the Bathurst Street bridge as a CN double-headed passenger train approaches. This photograph of the Toronto Terminals Railway yards was taken in the 1940s. The small former CN flat freight switching yard (now the GO Train storage yard) can be seen at left.

were very busy and dangerous to work in. The old cabin has watched many troop trains that passed in both world wars."

Probably the most comical control tower was the one at the Strachan Avenue level crossing. The square, glassed-in room thirty feet above ground perched on stilts. An approaching train triggered an alarm buzzer in the tower, which controlled an enormous brass gong whose sound must surely have been heard over the lake. No watchmen ever napped through that orchestration!

To relieve the monotony of lowering and raising gates, one of the watchmen planted window boxes with brilliant petunias and geraniums. He also dug up a bit of ground at the base of the tower for a cabbage patch. And they thrived!

One of the first recorded incidents of a train-and-car crash occurred when George Adams and his wife took their first and only drive in their snappy new touring car. Automobiles were still a novelty, licences were unheard of, and no one took driving lessons. The Adamses climbed into the front seat and after a few brief instructions they chugged happily through downtown Toronto. Suddenly, the railroad tracks at Strachan Avenue loomed into view and George realized that he did not know how to stop the car. After bumping over the first pair of tracks, the vehicle stalled. Annie and George jumped to safety just seconds before a heavy freight train smashed into their new car. The time between its purchase and its total destruction was under two hours!

The fascinating history of Toronto Terminals Railway, its property and buildings could fill volumes. The Union Station is a story in itself. Not even the impressive CN Tower could take its place as Toronto's most famous architectural landmark. Its formal opening was on August 6, 1927, when the popular Prince of Wales (who became King Edward VIII) cut the red ribbon and purchased the first train ticket issued at the new station.

Toronto Union Station, one of the greatest stations in North America, covers an entire city block. Its twenty-two limestone columns are forty feet tall and weigh more than seventy-five tons. Entering the Great Hall is a thrilling experience. Its magnificent arched ceiling rises eighty-eight feet above the marble floor. Its pillars and four-storey-high arched windows give one the feeling of being in a great temple. The spectacular and intricate architectural details throughout the station are a lasting tribute to its architects and builders.

Jake Charendoff worked as a red cap porter even before the new Union Station opened in 1927. He retired in January of 1974.

71

The nostalgic core of Toronto Union Station is kept alive in the memories of the millions of people who have passed through the station since its doors first opened. And what a kaleidoscope of memories!

Station staff in red caps hustled through the crowds. In the station's first decade, there were 125 staff members. Take-home pay varied from day to day and was often based on good luck. Only twelve men were on the payroll. They worked long hours but found time to organize a mouth-organ band, and the group became popular entertainers.

Jake Charendoff worked as a red cap even before the new station opened. When he retired on January 16, 1974, he felt he could have worked a few more years. There had never been a monotonous day for Jake. He loved people and the unpredictable life at the station. He never forgot the shock of being given a ten-cent tip by a titled Englishman after carrying the man's thirty-one pieces of luggage from the train to his suite at the Royal York Hotel.

When the late Madge Russell stepped off the boat-train on her arrival from Liverpool, she knew that Union Station was where she wanted to work. She was hired by the chef in the kitchen where food was prepared for station lunch counters. Madge's day began at 3 a.m., and the first chore of the day was to cook 3,500 donuts. By 8:30 in the morning she had also baked dozens of pies and prepared great stacks of cheese and ham sandwiches using the traditional Pullman loaves.

Strange items were frequently turned in to the station's lost-and-found room. One passenger actually forgot his canoe! Umbrellas, odd gloves, boots, eyeglasses and books were the most common articles left behind by travellers. No one ever claimed the seven-foot-tall forsythia bush that was turned in.

The constant changes in Toronto Terminals Railway yards and Union Station are distressing to lifelong Toronto residents. They miss the separate CPR and CNR ticket wickets, and the excitement if your ticket happened to be the long, accordion-folding type. Many families have fond recollections of lining up for excursion trains on holiday weekends, and of Saturday mornings in June when the station was filled with excited children going off to summer camps. And who could possibly forget the sepulchral voice from the loudspeaker that announced the arrival and departure of each train. It seemed to echo back and forth between walls and pillars, and somehow made you afraid that your train would leave before you reached the platform.

GRAND TRUNK RAILWAY.

THE PUBLIC ARE RESPECTFULLY IN-FORMED that the RAILWAY WILL BE OPENED THROUGH-OUT TO TORONTO,

On MONDAY, OCTOBER 27.

TRAINS WILL RUN AS FOLLOWS:

THROUGH TRAINS,

STOPPING AT ALL PRINCIPAL STATIONS,

Will leave MONTREAL every morning, (Sundays excepted,) at 7:30 A. M., arriving at TORONTO at 9:30 P. M.

Will leave TORONTO at 7:00 A. M., arriving at MONTREAL at 9:00 P. M.

LOCAL TRAINS,

STOPPING AT STATIONS,

Will leave BROCKVILLE, daily, for MONTREAL, at 8:30, A. M.; returning from MONTREAL at 8:30, P. M.

Will leave BELLEVILLE, daily, for BROCKVILLE, at 7:00, A. M. returning from BROCKVILLE at 3:15, P. M.

Will leave COBOURG, daily, for TORONTO, at 6:30, A. M.; returning from TORONTO at 4:45, P. M

The Trains will be run on Montreal Time, which is—
8½ Minutes faster than Brockville Time.

12	"	"	Kingston	"
14½	"	"	Belleville	"
23	"	"	Toronto	"

Freight Trains will not run between Brockville and Toronto during the first week.

Fares between Toronto and Montreal :

First Class......................... .... $10 00
Second do................................. 8 00

S. P. BIDDER,
General Manager,

Montreal, October 18, 1856. 1025

A copy of the first Grand Trunk timetable for the opening of the Montreal–Toronto line on October 27, 1856.

Today, a unique aura still surrounds Toronto Union Station, one unaltered by time and structural changes, one that can be experienced each time you step inside the Great Hall.

In this photograph, circa 1920, paper rolls are unloaded from a thirty-five-foot wooden-sided CN boxcar.
Photographer unknown

Construction of the CN Tower as seen from the Bathurst Street bridge.

When Wiarton's passenger service was discontinued in the 1960s, the station was boarded up and its future became uncertain. Enthusiastic support of the Wiarton Parks Board and a generous grant made it possible for the station to be moved to Wiarton Bluewater Park in 1971.

WIARTON

The town of Wiarton was settled at the southern tip of Colpoys Bay on Georgian Bay, in 1856. The two modes of public transportation available at that time were a steamboat named *Champion,* which made daily trips to Owen Sound, and a stagecoach service. A quarter of a century later, Wiarton became a town at the "end of the rail."

It was the Grand Trunk Railway that brought the line into Wiarton, but the ownership of the railway had changed hands several times en route. The first chartered company began construction in 1855, with its starting point at Port Dover on Lake Erie. By the time the tracks finally entered Wiarton in November 1881, the line was owned completely by the Grand Trunk Railroad.

A newspaper recorded the event, saying, "A new era of prosperity and activity seems to have been inaugurated by the extension of the 'modern civilization to this fair section of the country.'"

The splendid reception that traditionally accompanied the arrival of a town's first train was noticeably missing. The train arrived at 6 p.m. on November 21, 1881, with its passengers sitting on rough benches fastened to the floor of an open flatcar. Engineer Joshua Wilson and train conductor William Cook drank a few mugs of beer with the welcoming committee, then headed back to Palmerston. Regular passenger service began in the spring of 1882.

Another small company planned to bring its railway to the area. This was the short-lived Saugeen Valley Railway Company. However, before construction began, their charter was withdrawn.

After the arrival of the Grand Trunk, Wiarton wondered just how long they would have to put up with the makeshift station which stood behind one of the town's popular hotels. It was said to resemble a crude packing box. Visitors arriving in town on the train were shocked by its appearance. The owners of Wiarton's furniture factories, whose thriving business was profitable for the railway, felt they deserved a more dignified station.

In the early 1900s this depressing shanty was replaced with a magnificent new station. An ornate octagonal turret rose above the roof line, and a two-storey tower was built above the entrance. Intricately carved gingerbread fretwork crowned the gable of the roof. The large circular waiting room was a joy to passengers awaiting the arrival of their train.

When Wiarton's passenger service was discontinued in the 1960s, the station was boarded up and its future became uncertain. Fortunately, through enthusiastic support of the Parks Board and a generous grant, the station was moved to Wiarton Bluewater Park in 1971. The building has been beautifully renovated and serves as a popular recreation centre for park visitors.

WIARTON AND SOUTHAMPTON TO PALMERSTON.

TRAINS NORTH											TRAINS SOUTH					
SECOND CLASS		FIRST CLASS				Station to Station	STATIONS.	Telegraph Offices.	From Port Dover.	From Harriston.	FIRST CLASS				SECOND CLASS	
12	10	8	6	4	2			D. day / N. night			1	3	5	7	9	11
Mixed.	Mixed.	Passenger.	Passenger.	Passenger.	Passenger.	Mls.			Mls.		Passenger.	Passenger.	Passenger.	Passenger.	Mixed.	Mixed.
P.M. 12.10				P.M. 11.50	P.M. 5.50		Arr.....**Wiarton**.....Dep.	D	167.5		A.M. 5.20	A.M. 9.00				P.M. 2.25
11.53				†11.39	‡5.35	4.9	Clavering		162.6		†5.32	†9.15				2.45
11.40				11.31	5.25	3.3	Hepworth	D	159.3		5.41	9.28				3.20
11.05				†11.24	‡5.12	2.4	Park Head		156.9		†5.47	†9.36				3.40
10.45				11.13	4.58	4.5	Allenford	D	152.4		5.58	9.55				4.00
10.20				10.58	4.40	5.2	Tara & Invermay	D	147.2		6.13	10.20				4.40
9.55				†10.45	4.20	5.5	Dobbington		141.7		†6.26	10.35				5.05
9.30				10.26	4.00	7.3	**Chesley**	D	134.4		6.45	11.05				5.45
8.50				10.15	3.45	4.4	Elmwood	D	130.0		6.55	11.20				6.10
8.25				10.00	3.25	6.3	Hanover	D	123.7		7.11	11.45				6.40
7.55				9.43	3.05	6.3	Neustadt	D	117.4		7.26	P.M. 12.10				7.05
7.35				9.33	2.53	3.8	Ayton	D	113.6		7.35	12.25				7.35
7.00				†9.25	*2.38	2.3	Alsfeldt		111.3		†7.42	†12.35				†7.46
6.48				†9.17	†2.28	2.8	Drew		108.5		†7.50	†12.47				†7.58
6.30				9.05	2.15	5.0	Dep.....**Harriston**.....Arr.	D	103.5		8.01	1.02				8.15
		P.M. 11.15	P.M. 4.35				Arr.....**Southampton**.....Dep.	D		128.5			A.M. 6.00	A.M. 9.35		
		11.05	4.20			4.3	Port Elgin	D		124.2			6.08	10.00		
		*10.51	3.55			5.5	Turners			118.8			†6.20	10.15		
	P.M. 12.55	10.32	3.30			7.2	Paisley	D		111.5			6.36	10.45	P.M. 2.30	
	12.35	10.17	3.12			6.4	Pinkerton			105.1			6.50	11.02	3.12	
	12.25	10.14	3.09			1.4	Cargill	D		103.8			6.54	11.06	3.30	
	P.M. 12.08	*10.08	3.03			2.7	Dunkeld			101.0			7.00	11.15	3.45	
	d11.50 a11.20	9.57	2.53			4.5	Walkerton	D		96.5			7.13	11.40	a4.05 d4.30	
	11.00	9.42	2.38			6.0	Mildmay	D		90.5			7.26	11.58	5.05	
	10.10	9.21	2.16			8.8	Clifford	D		81.8			7.46	P.M. 12.25	6.00	
6.20	9.35	9.05	2.00	9.05	2.15	6.7	Arr.....**Harriston**.....Dep.	D	103.5	75.0	8.01	1.05	8.01	12.50	7.00	8.20
6.00 A.M.	8.50 A.M.	8.50 P.M.	1.45 P.M.	8.50 P.M.	2.00 P.M.	5.5	Dep.....**Palmerston**.....Arr.	D / N	98.4	69.5	8.15 A.M.	1.25 P.M.	8.15 A.M.	1.05 P.M.	7.20 P.M.	8.40 P.M.
12	10	8	6	4	2						1	3	5	7	9	11

Any train failing to arrive at Southampton or Wiarton on time, must keep clear of all trains of a like or superior class that may be due to leave. See Rules Nos. 48, 49 and 57.

*Do not stop: see Rule No. 35.   † Flag Stations; Trains stop for passengers.   Railway Crossing near Harriston; see Rule No. 112.

NOTE.—Trains Nos. 1 and 4 will run on Mondays, Wednesdays and Fridays only, between Wiarton and Palmerston.

Trains Nos. 5 and 8 will run on Tuesdays, Thursdays and Saturdays only, between Southampton and Palmerston.

All other regular trains run daily, Sundays excepted.

A copy of CN employees' timetable showing the passenger train schedule between Wiarton and Harriston, and Southampton and Harriston.

WOODSTOCK

When the Royal Train arrived in Woodstock at 11 a.m. on October 22, 1919, few housewives were concerned about their families' noonday dinner! The Prince of Wales—everyone's idol—would be in town for one hour and nothing else mattered. But back in 1853, when the very first train ever to arrive in Woodstock made its appearance, it was an all-male welcoming committee that turned out. The ladies wisely decided that this celebration was for the men. And how right they were!

Upon the completion of the first section of the Great Western Railway between Hamilton and London, company officials felt a celebration was in order. A special train left Hamilton at 9:30 a.m. on December 15, picking up dignitaries at communities along the line. Woodstock's station, gaily decorated with flags and bunting, was the scene of much merriment all morning. Tables set out on the platform were laden with great platters of sandwiches and a generous supply of whisky and champagne. Well-wishers toasted the railway's directors, the royal family, railroad labourers, and anyone else whose name came to mind. Woodstock's dignitaries then climbed aboard the train and joined in the fun with other passengers who were eager to get to London for the big celebration.

Reporters covering the festivities at the London Exchange Hotel spoke well of the decorations, the top-hatted railway officials, and the imported lobster, but as for the toasts and "refreshments," their comment was, "The less said the better."

Just twenty years prior to the construction of this railway, Woodstock consisted of one tavern, a small store and a few houses. It was regarded as being "little less than a wilderness." By 1853 the population had grown to over a thousand residents and two hundred houses had been built. The town could boast of having two railways when the little Port Dover & Lake Huron Railway built its line through Woodstock on its route to Stratford in 1874. Both companies used the same station. Before the turn of the century, the CPR line running between Toronto and Windsor also passed through Woodstock. This company had its own station.

Woodstock's railway station has been in use for well over a hundred years, having been built before the amalgamation of the Great Western Railway with the Grand Trunk Railway in 1882. It has always been regarded as one of southern Ontario's most handsome stations.

It is approached from the north by crossing a narrow bridge which spans many tracks. Since the opening of the little bridge, generations of train-lovers have used it as an exciting observation point. Even though coal- or wood-burning locomotives, with their shrill, musical steam whistles, are a thing of the past, it's still a thrill to lean against the railing and watch the constant activity around the yards. And it's the best place to catch one's first view of the historic station!

Obviously, this grand old two-storey brick station with all its embellishments was created by craftsmen whose goal was perfection in every detail. Over the years, restoration and the many layers of exterior paint have concealed much of the station's early charm, but the basic design of the original station still remains. The railroad was a man's world in the 1920s. Few positions were held by women. One of the lucky few employed by the railway in Woodstock was a young farm girl named Beryl Hart, who was just four feet eleven inches tall. Beryl became an efficient telegraph operator at the station and trained many other girls in this important field. One of her jobs as an operator was to keep the batteries in working order. Eleanor Gardhouse, daughter of the late Beryl Hart, recalls that the two large two-gallon jars were kept filled with water and bluestone. A copper "frog" (a device resembling a frog) was suspended in the liquid. A wire from the "frog" travelled to the instruments, providing the power. Care had to be taken not to splash

Woodstock's historic station has been in use for well over a hundred years. It was built prior to the amalgamation of the Great Western and the Grand Trunk in 1882.

this solution onto one's clothes.

One of the high points in Beryl Hart's career as a telegrapher was taking the message when the famous racehorse Man O' War won the race which set a new world record on July 11, 1920. Hart became manager of the telegraph office at the Woodstock station and in 1928 married Russell Adams, a CNR expressman.

Beginning in 1881, Woodstock residents could set their clocks by the punctual passage of the speedy, early morning mail train chartered by the Toronto *Globe and Mail*. This train pulled out of Toronto at 3:55 a.m., dropped off bundles of newspapers at communities along its line, and arrived promptly at 6:40 a.m. in London. Old CN locomotive #702's shrieking steam whistle served the town of Woodstock as a faithful alarm clock for twenty years.

(above)
Woodstock station circa 1885.
Photographer unknown

(below)
Woodstock station circa 1919.
E. Gardhouse collection

CPR 136, a 4-4-0 type built in 1883, running on a railfan trip to Owen Sound in the mid-1970s with CP 1057, a 4-6-0 type. This photograph was taken near Fraxa, just west of Orangeville. Both engines are part of the South Simcoe Railway at Tottenham. CPR 136 was recently returned to weekend tourist-train service.

Aultsville Station at Upper Canada Village. This photograph shows a typical
Grand Trunk train with a 2-6-0 engine, a baggage-mail car and a passenger car.

Port McNicoll station, Canadian Pacific Railway.

Apple Hill station, Canadian Pacific Railway. This station is on the original
Ontario & Quebec line west of Montreal to Smiths Falls.

Hanover station, Grand Trunk Railway.

Walkerton station, Grand Trunk Railway.

Southampton station, Grand Trunk Railway.

Dundas station, Grand Trunk Railway.

Huntsville station, CN-owned at
the time of this photograph.

Bracebridge station, CN-owned at
the time of this photograph.

Havelock station, Canadian Pacific Railway.

Kingsville station, Pere Marquette Railroad.

Campbellford station, built by the Grand Trunk but owned by CN at the
time of this photograph.

Ridgeway station.

Washago station and water tower.

EPILOGUE

In the exciting years of the grand old steam locomotives, almost any time was train time! This era once seemed as permanent as anything could be.

Century-old Ontario maps show scores of branch lines fanning out in every direction from main lines of the Grand Trunk and the Canadian Pacific. Most towns along these local lines owed their success to the railroad, and their survival depended upon continuation of railway service. It was their link with the outside world. It is impossible to guess how many small stations existed at one time. Many were spaced at ten-mile intervals.

The social life of a community centred around its station. Although the entertainment was unsophisticated, it had variety which appealed to everyone.

If you indulge in nostalgic dreams of the days of steam locomotives, you recall the exhilarating sound of the whistle. It could also be a comforting sound in the isolation of winter, assuring you that all was well with the train crew.

Yes, it is good to have known that time. Who would have thought that, before long, four-lane highways would bring about so many changes? Half a century ago, no one predicted that our generation would have to visit a museum to see a steam locomotive! I miss those grand old trains, and the railway stations, and the railway men who so generously shared with me their memories of the busy years.

When I drive through rural Ontario today, I often discover traces of old railways. The saddest sight I can think of is an abandoned branch line. I have strolled along old roadbeds and imagined hearing the sound of an approaching wayfreight. It's easy to visualize the old red caboose disappearing down the track on its last trip.

Will it ever return?

INDEX OF RAILWAY COMPANIES

Drawing by C.W. Kettlewell of Jerseyville station, Westfield Pioneer Village.